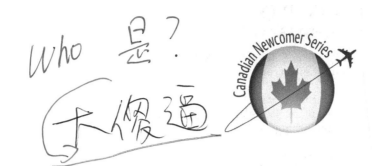

Who 是?
天假逼

D0118305

You're Hired...
Now What?

An Immigrant's Guide to Success in the Canadian Workplace

WORKBOOK

Beverley Payne   **Terry Webb**

Illustrated by Sarah Jane Payne

OXFORD
UNIVERSITY PRESS

OXFORD

UNIVERSITY PRESS

8 Sampson Mews, Suite 204, Don Mills, Ontario M3C 0H5
www.oupcanada.com

Oxford University Press is a department of the University of Oxford.
It furthers the University's objective of excellence in research, scholarship,
and education by publishing worldwide in

Oxford   New York

Auckland   Cape Town   Dar es Salaam   Hong Kong   Karachi
Kuala Lumpur   Madrid   Melbourne   Mexico City   Nairobi
New Delhi   Shanghai   Taipei   Toronto

With offices in
Argentina   Austria   Brazil   Chile   Czech Republic   France   Greece
Guatemala   Hungary   Italy   Japan   Poland   Portugal   Singapore
South Korea   Switzerland   Thailand   Turkey   Ukraine   Vietnam

Oxford is a trade mark of Oxford University Press
in the UK and in certain other countries

Published in Canada
by Oxford University Press

Library and Archives Canada Cataloguing in Publication

Payne, Beverley, 1950-
You're hired—now what? : workbook : how to survive
and thrive at a Canadian job / Beverley Payne, Terry Webb.

(Canadian newcomer series)

ISBN 978-0-19-543219-0

1. Business etiquette--Canada. 2. Immigrants—Employment—
Canada. 3. Courtesy in the workplace. I. Webb, Terry, 1955–
II. Title. III. Series: Canadian newcomer series

HD8108.5.A2G65 2009 Suppl.   650.1'3   C2008-908101-3

Cover image: istockphoto.com/Claire Desjardins

This book is printed on permanent acid-free paper.
Printed and bound in Canada.

10 11 12 - 18 17 16

Introduction

Welcome to the *You're Hired...Now What? Workbook!* The chapters of this workbook follow the themes and key points from *You're Hired...Now What*. This, however, is only the beginning: the workbook also introduces additional concepts and is designed to take you from an understanding of the new ideas you are learning about the Canadian workplace to an application of this knowledge through activities and interaction.

Here's what you will find in each chapter:

Key point focus
Point-form summary of the key points in the text

First things first
- Introduction to the chapter's theme
- Opportunity to develop reading skills
- Activities based on an extension of the reading or in preparation for the dialogue

Buzzwords
- Practice of buzzwords encountered in *You're Hired...Now What?* plus additional relevant idioms
- Vocabulary enhancement

Language patterns
- Examination of the structure of language patterns and collocations
- Use of the patterns learned

Vocabulary
- Words from *You're Hired...Now What?* as well as new vocabulary based upon the unit theme
- Opportunity to expand language for workplace communication

Dialogue
- Oral communication patterns
- Contextualized fluency and pronunciation practice
- Language development for common workplace communication needs

Writing
- Activities geared to the Canadian Language Benchmarks (CLBs) 5 to 8

Group work
- Interactive small-group activities that encourage the use of the chapter's vocabulary and language patterns

On Your Own
- Individual research and reflection
- Self-assessment of language progress and identification of future learning goals

Contents

Chapter 1

How to Work Well in Canada

Key Point Focus

- Business culture
- Being open to new ideas
- Workplace values

First things first

The *Oxford ESL Dictionary* defines *culture* as "the customs, ideas, and civilization, etc. of a particular society or group of people."

Understanding business culture and communication patterns in the Canadian workplace can involve a steep learning curve for many new immigrants. Canada covers a large geographical area, and you may observe regional differences in some cultural practices as you travel from place to place. Although there are federal and provincial regulations that provide laws and guidelines for working Canadians, each company will also have some of its own customs, practices, and workplace values. And just like Canada does, each workplace contains a mix of cultural practices.

Trying to observe and understand culture is like trying to observe and understand an iceberg. There are things that are easy to see on the surface. However, it is not so easy to understand and predict what is under the surface. Values are sets of beliefs about the way people should behave with one another. Sometimes these values are easy to see and other times they seem to be very challenging to understand.

Anyone who is either looking for a job or starting out in a new job will require some time to figure out the expectations, culture, and customs of any new or prospective workplace. Meeting new people and learning about a new workplace culture can be difficult.

Exercise A

Working with a partner, discuss your observations about the following workplace values. Which values are similar to those of your native culture and which values are different?

Canadian Workplace Values	Values That Are Similar to Those in My Native Country	Values That Are Different from Those in My Native Country
Communication • Direct expression of your ideas • Politeness and diplomacy • Use of personal space		
Equality • Legislation for equity • Same job types and positions for men and women		
Self-direction • Expectation of individual initiative • Ability to problem solve • Ability to work on individual projects		
Teamwork • Ability to collaborate and communicate with others • Ability to share ideas and tasks		
Time • Time-wasting not acceptable • Keeping to a schedule • Beginning meetings at a specified time • Being on time		
Informality • Use of first names • Business casual clothing at many workplaces • Few formal rituals • Greeting can be a wave, a handshake, or a hello		
Self-Improvement • Attending workshops • Taking classes		

Exercise B

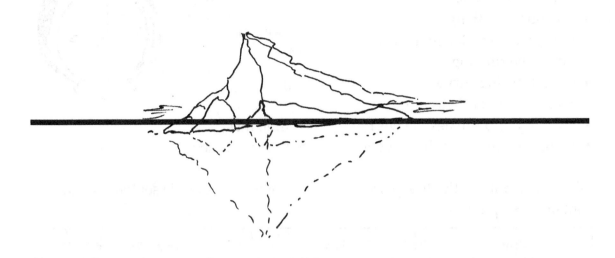

1. Above the line, make a list of the Canadian workplace values and customs that are easily seen.
2. Below the line, make a list of the values and customs that seem confusing and are not as easy to understand.
3. Working in small groups, compare and discuss the workplace value observations you have made.

Exercise C

In pairs, complete the following.

1. How would you explain the two concepts below? Do you live to work or do you work to live? Mark an X to show where you would place yourself on this scale. Discuss your response with your partner.

LIVE TO WORK   WORK TO LIVE

_____

_____

2. Complete these sentences.

   Work in Canada is … _____

   Work is … _____

   My career is … _____

   My hope is … _____

Buzzwords

- don't beat around the bush
- do your own thing
- many hands make light work
- out of the running
- steep learning curve
- take you under their wing
- the early bird catches the worm
- there is no time like the present

Add your own drawing to this clock to illustrate one of the *time* buzz-words.

- time flies
- time is money

Fill in the blanks with phrases from the list above and example sentences that contain these phrases.

Definition	Phrase	Example Sentence
1. Large tasks become smaller when the work is shared by many people.	Many hands make light work.	*We've got a big job to do today, but …*
2. Be direct in your communication		*I would like to understand, please don't …*
3. Do what you want or think is best		*I might do it differently, but I know you will …*
4. Time passes very quickly		
5. Time is valuable and should not be wasted		
6. Not able to participate		

Language patterns

Asking for help

Would you and *could you* are both polite forms that can be used to make requests and ask permission. *Can you* is also used to make informal requests; however, it sounds less polite.

Exercise A

Complete the following sentences.

Could

Could you recommend <u>*a good place to buy a computer*</u> ?

Could you recommend _____ ?

Could you tell me a little more about _____ ?

Could you please _____ ?

Would

Would it be possible to *fax this report* _____ ?

Would it be possible to _____ ?

Would you be able to _____ ?

Exercise B

Working with a partner, use the *could / would* sentence patterns to ask each other for help with, or information about, the following:

- finding a new apartment
- finding a doctor
- good restaurants

- making an international phone call
- team meetings
- Canadian business culture

Vocabulary

aggressive	equality	rituals
annoyed	minimize	task
collaborative	oblivious	valuable
customs	promptness	values
embarrassment		

Use five of the vocabulary words to write an email to a friend about Canadian workplace values.

Share your email with a partner. Then, discuss the definitions of any vocabulary words that you did not use in your email.

Dialogue

Elizabeth	Arti	Farjar

Elizabeth: Welcome! Please come in.

Arti: Thank you.

Elizabeth: Did you have any difficulty finding my home?

Arti: No. Not at all. Your directions were very clear.

Elizabeth: Oh good. We were just beginning to get a little worried about you.

Arti: Worried?

Farjar: Worried? I am not sure I understand.

Elizabeth: Oh, I understand how time flies. We are all just glad you arrived here safely. Go ahead into the living room while I take care of your coats.

Arti: Farjar, does Elizabeth seem a little anxious to you?

Farjar: Yes, she does. She also seems a bit annoyed.

Arti: I wonder what she meant by *time flies*?

Exercise A

Working with a partner, discuss the dialogue.

1. Why was Elizabeth anxious? _____

   _____

2. What values might be involved? _____

   _____

Writing

CLB 5

Write a 150-word paragraph about equality in the Canadian workplace.

CLB 6

Write a 250-word paragraph about equality in the Canadian workplace. Include one specific example of workplace equality.

CLB 7

Write a 350-word paragraph about equality in the Canadian workplace. Include two specific examples of workplace equality.

CLB 8

Write a 3-paragraph, 500-word report about equality in the Canadian workplace. Include three specific examples of workplace equality.

Group work

Canadian Business Concept: Work is a high priority for most Canadians, and many people work overtime and on weekends to complete their work.

Exercise A

1. Discuss the similarities and differences in the amount of time that people from various cultures spend at work and commuting. Do you find anything unusual about this aspect of Canadian work culture?

2. Based on what you have experienced so far in Canada, would you agree or disagree with the Canadian Business Concept above?

Use these expression patterns to state your opinions.

Agree	Disagree
That sounds right because ...	I don't think that sounds right because ...
I agree that ...	I disagree because ...
That's probably right because ...	I find it hard to agree because ...

Give some examples to support your responses.

Exercise B

In small groups, select a sentence from the box below. How would you explain the meaning of this sentence? How does it relate to Canadian workplace values? What is your reaction to the sentence?

Time is money.
Canadians are time conscious.
The early bird catches the worm.
Call me Fred. We don't use the
    Mr. very much around here.

Thank you for the flowers and get-well
    card.
Many hands make light work.
There is no time like the present.
Don't beat around the bush.

Exercise C

Equality in the workplace is not just about gender. It also involves race, age, religious background, and physical ability. What are your experiences and observations about workplace equality in your native country? Compare this to what you have observed in Canada.

On your own

Watch a TV program that takes place in a workplace environment (ask your friends or your teacher for suggestions). What customs and values did you notice? Share your observations with your classmates.

Do an online search for *Equality in the Canadian Workplace*. Take notes on the information you find. Share your notes with your classmates.

Personal learning: practising English outside of the classroom

Keep your own record of your communication goals, progress, and reactions to new concepts. Review it weekly to help you chart your progress.

Canadian business culture is ... _____

Today I learned ... _____

By next class I will use this learning by ... _____

Chapter 2

Understanding Your Workplace Culture

Key Point Focus

- Industry and company cultures
- Communicating using acronyms, unwritten rules, and buzzwords
- Observing and gathering information

First things first

Generally, when you start a new job, you will be given an orientation package or asked to attend an orientation session. All of the new information about policies and protocols may seem a little intimidating, but these written guidelines are meant to help with the successful transition into a company.

"If your company runs an orientation session, go!" says Shelly Brown, President of Bromelin People Practices. "Many employees don't bother. This is a mistake. The orientation session is critical to integrating into the company. If you are given materials about the company in the first few days, be sure to read them. If you are not given information on the company's products, ask for it."

Many company rules, however, are not written down. In fact, your new co-workers may not even be able to identify any unwritten rules for you. To people who have worked for the same employer for a long time, these rules or norms are just parts of the accepted practices. For example, in some workplaces people may be expected to take their full break then return at the exact minute they are due back. In other workplaces, breaks may often be cut short because of work pressures. Taking breaks, calling in sick, and scheduling time off are a few of the areas in which you might observe unwritten rules. Understanding the unwritten rules requires observation, perception, dialogue, and patience.

Exercise A

In pairs, discuss what you have observed and heard about the following situations. How do your co-workers behave in these situations?

Situation	Timing How long do people take for this activity? Is there a specific amount of time allowed? Is it done on the dot?	Observations What do your co-workers do in this situation? How does this compare with other cultures?
Morning break		
Lunch		
Afternoon break		
End of workday		
Greeting co-workers		
Add your own situation _____		

Exercise B

In groups of three or four, compare your observations and opinions about the skills required to fit into a new work situation. Which skills are the same for many jobs? Which skills are very specific? Do you notice any patterns?

Work Situation	Skills Required (Person 1)	Skills Required (Person 2)	Skills Required (Person 3)	Skills Required (Person 4)
Retail merchandising	*people skills, good at talking with people*			
Customer service				
Office				
Manufacturing				
Food processing				
Restaurant				
Education and community services				
Add your own work situation _____				

Exercise C

In groups of three or four, discuss your own experiences with job orientation. Were you given adequate introductions, information, and guidelines? Was another employee assigned to help you? What would you suggest to improve the process for people whose first language is not English?

Buzzwords

Match each term or expression with its meaning and then use it in a sentence.

a)	24/7	f)	new hire
b)	bottom line	g)	on the dot
c)	figure out	h)	round-the-clock service
d)	fit in	i)	slacking off
e)	learn the ropes	j)	you bet

1. __ I agree with you _____
   _____

2. __ understand the procedures _____
   _____

3. __ work easily with a group of people _____
   _____

4. __ find the answer to something _____
   _____

5. __ all the time (24 hours a day, 7 days a week) _____
   _____

6. __ service help 24 hours a day _____
   _____

7. __ punctual _____
   _____

8. __ someone who just got a job _____
   _____

9. __ not working hard _____
   _____

10. __ the important conclusion _____
    _____

Language patterns

The Oxford *Phrasal Verbs* dictionary identifies *fit in* as a key phrasal verb.

Use a phrasal verbs dictionary to look up some uses for *fit in*. Complete the chart.

Describe the use of *fit in*.	Write a sentence using *fit in*.
to live or work easily with a group of people.	*I hope I will fit in with my new colleagues at work.*

Vocabulary

Write a clear definition for each of these words.

1. protocol: _____
2. intimidating: _____
3. transition: _____
4. ritual: _____
5. cubicle: _____
6. procedure: _____
7. uncertain: _____
8. formal: _____
9. culture: _____
10. informal: _____
11. critical: _____
12. trend: _____
13. clarify: _____
14. acronym: _____
15. norm: _____

Compare your definitions with a partner's. Use a dictionary to look up any new words.

Using eight of the vocabulary words, write a paragraph describing your first week with your new employer. If you are still seeking employment, write a paragraph about what you might expect to happen during your first week on a new job. Use eight of the vocabulary words.

Dialogue

Anne   Chen

Anne: Hello. You're new here aren't you? My name
        is Anne. Welcome to the company.
Chen: Thank you. My name is Chen.
Anne: What department are you in?
Chen: I am in finance. My supervisor is Ms Rampaul.
Anne: Oh yes. And how are you settling in?
Chen: Just fine, thank you. But sometimes I find it hard to understand what
        people are talking about. I am uncertain about what they are trying to
        tell me. It is as if they are using another language and it is not English.
Anne: Yes, I know what you mean. Many people use acronyms as short forms
        for longer words or groups of words. It is hard to catch everything the
        first time you hear it.
Chen: That could be it, but I do not really know what you mean.
Anne: Have you heard about the new CPP forms in HR?
Chen: Yes, that is my problem. That did not make any sense to me.
Anne: I would be glad to help clarify and "translate" for you. My cubicle is just
        over there by the window.
Chen: Thank you so much. That would be a great help.
Anne: You're welcome. Any time. I've got to run now. Good luck, Chen!
Chen: Thanks again, Anne.

Writing

CLB 5

Write a 150-word letter to a friend, telling him or her about a meeting you attended.

CLB 6

Take notes during a meeting. Make a list of questions you would like to ask.

CLB 7

Take notes during a meeting. Using your notes, write a paragraph about your
understanding of the main focus of the meeting. Remember to include an
introduction, supporting points, and a conclusion

CLB 8

Do some online research of the topic of *Workplace Meeting Protocol*. Describe and
summarize your findings in a four-paragraph essay. Remember to include an
introduction, develop your main points, and finish with a conclusion. Create a one-
paragraph summary of your findings to be shared verbally with your classmates.

Group work

Exercise A

In pairs, create short dialogues to check and clarify information about four of the following:

- The location of meeting rooms
- Workplace traditions
- Location of the lunchroom
- The purpose of an upcoming meeting
- The Victoria Day holiday

Phrase to Clarify Information	Dialogue
Sorry, I didn't catch that.	A: The Health and Safety Committee is meeting in the Northwest Room. B: Sorry, I didn't catch that. Which room is the meeting in? A: The Northwest Room.
I'm afraid I didn't catch that.	
Could you please repeat that?	
I'm sorry, could you please repeat that?	

Exercise B

> Every company has its own rules for when employees should call in sick. Some companies don't want employees spreading germs, and employees are encouraged to take off time for a bad cold. In other companies, you have to be seriously ill to take a day off. Find out your company's policies and workplace culture, and use your good judgment to make the final decision.

In small groups, discuss company protocols for calling in sick. In what way are the expectations in Canada the same as or different from those in other cultures?

Exercise C

In pairs, discuss the protocol at your workplaces for arranging doctor and dentist visits. If you do not know, what would be the best way to find out? Create a role play in which one of you asks the other about medical visit protocol.

Exercise D

In small groups, discuss employee benefits. Did you consider employee benefits when you were looking for a job, or was salary the main consideration?

On your own

Complete the chart, then add any additional acronyms that you have heard in the workplace. Write example sentences using the acronyms.

Acronym	Meaning	Example sentence
HR	Human Resources	You will need to get your documents back to HR by tomorrow.
CEO		
ASAP		
ROI		
CPP		
WHMIS		

Use a notebook to keep a log of the acronyms that you hear.

Read your company's orientation handbook. Does it include a glossary of acronyms?

Personal learning: practising English outside of the classroom

This past week I ... _____

Tomorrow I will try ... _____

My favourite new word is ... _____

By next class I will ... _____

Chapter 3

Setting the Stage for Success

Key Point Focus

- Making a great first impression
- Getting to know people on your team and in other parts of the company
- What your company and your boss want from you

First things first

Making a great first impression is vital to your success on the job. As a newcomer to Canada and, most likely, to the English language, your nervousness will probably cause you to talk too quickly. Keep your speaking rate down. Talk at the same pace and volume level as the person you are speaking to. Focus your attention on listening to this individual. Your new acquaintance deserves 100 percent of your attention. This will also take the pressure off you and give you time to compose yourself.

Develop your small-talk skills. As someone who is a skilled small-talker, you will come across as an open and friendly person. Be careful not to overdo it, though, or people may find you annoying and too chatty.

  You may feel uncomfortable looking directly at the other person. However, in Canada, when you meet someone for the first time you should look right into that person's eyes. This is very important. Making eye contact conveys confidence and self-assurance. It indicates an interest in the other person.

Your body language will speak louder than words. Stand tall, smile, make eye contact, and greet each person you meet with a firm handshake. Both you and the other person will feel more at ease.

Exercise A

Canadian Business Concept: Canadians shake hands firmly when they meet. If you aren't comfortable shaking hands, smile and nod, and say, "It's not my custom to shake hands, but I am very pleased to meet you."

Survey your peers to find out how people are greeted in other countries. What do people do to make a good first impression?

Exercise B

Match each picture with the message it gives:

1. _____

2. _____

3. _____

4. _____

5. _____

6. _____

7. _____

a) Hello. Nice to see you.
b) Are you serious? Is this true?
c) I don't know. Whatever …
d) I'm happy today.

e) I'm worried about something.
f) I'm trying to solve a problem.
g) I'm angry about something.

In small groups, discuss the physical clues that helped you to determine the messages.

Exercise C

In small groups, discuss three gestures you use frequently and explain what they mean. Which gestures are impolite in your culture? What are your observations about body language in Canada? How do these differ from observations about your own culture? What can you learn about people from their body language?

Exercise D

In pairs, discuss the differences in work cultures and communication styles between your native culture and Canada. How could these differences affect your job in Canada? How might these lead to miscommunication? How might these affect team building in your company?

Exercise E

In small groups, discuss what you would do to prepare for your first days on the job. What strategies could you use to familiarize yourself with your work environment? What office routines would you establish? What are some of the important things you need to learn about in the first days on the job? What concerns will you need to address during your first days on the job?

Exercise F

 Canadian Business Concept: Being efficient and organized will go a long way toward helping you succeed in Canada.

What does this mean? How would you implement this concept in your job?

Buzzwords

Match the expressions with the appropriate meanings below, then use each expression in a sentence. Not all expressions will be used.

a)	bash	i)	pad your account
b)	be proactive	j)	punch a clock
c)	bigwig	k)	slacker
d)	brownie points	l)	start off on the right foot
e)	have the executives' ears	m)	stressing you out
f)	in the loop	n)	traffic jam
g)	office etiquette	o)	twiddle your thumbs
h)	operating at warp speed		

1. __ take initiative _____

_____

2. __ aware of _____

_____

3. __ be on your best behaviour _____

_____

4. __ party or social gathering _____

    _____

5. __ inflate your expenses _____

    _____

6. __ be listened to by the executives _____

    _____

Language patterns

Complete the definitions and then use each *up* term in a sentence.

1. write up: *write an account of* _____
    Eva is going to be written up for coming in late all the time.

2. keep up: _____

    _____

3. think up: _____

    _____

4. set up: _____

    _____

5. speak up: _____

    _____

6. call up: _____

    _____

Vocabulary

Discuss the following vocabulary with your classmates.

acquaintance	feedback	procedures
contribution	flexible	tip
established	performance review	vital

Look at the following pairs of sentences and decide whether the pairs have the same or different meanings.

1. a) Employers often conduct employee assessments to evaluate the employees' work.
    b) Employers often conduct performance reviews on their employees.

2. a) It is insignificant whether you confirm the appointment time or not.
    b) It is vital that you confirm the appointment time.

3. a) No one noticed the stranger approaching the reception desk.
    b) No one noticed the acquaintance approaching the reception desk.

4. a) The Hudson's Bay Company was founded in 1670.
   b) The Hudson's Bay Company was established in 1670.

5. a) The information about WHMIS is posted in the materials room.
   b) The procedures about WHMIS are posted in the materials room.

6. a) The feedback she received from her employer was constructive.
   b) The assessment she received from her employer was constructive.

7. a) She was honoured for her contributions to the contract.
   b) She was honoured for her promotion to the contract.

8. a) In some countries, it is not acceptable to tip workers.
   b) In some countries, it is not acceptable to shout at workers.

9. a) Accommodating employees with physical challenges is a priority in the company.
   b) Assimilating employees with physical challenges is a priority in the company.

10. a) You will have more success in your job if you prove to be flexible.
    b) You will have more success in your job if you prove to be adaptable.

Dialogue

Fill in the blanks using words from the Buzzwords and Vocabulary sections.

Alex	Eva

Alex: Hi, Eva. How's it going?

Eva: Not so well. I just had my first ₁ _Performance review_ with the company ₂ _big wig_ . I don't think he will give me a good write up.

Alex: You're a hard worker. I'm sure you did just fine.

Eva: I'm not so sure. He said that I took long lunches. Alex, I always ₃ _punch a clock_ when I go anywhere. I was only late getting back from lunch one time. The roads were really busy. I got held up in a ₄ _traffic jam_ .

Alex: That's too bad. Did he not give you any positive ₅ _feed back_ ? Surely, he complimented you on your ₆ _contribution_ to the company.

Eva: He seemed to focus on making sure that I understood company ₇ _procedures_ .

Alex: I understand your confusion. I like to do my job and do it well. But my supervisor just told me that he has a hard time keeping up with me. He says I'm 8 *operating at warp speed*. It's 9 *stressing me* out. What am I supposed to do? 10 *to twiddle my thumbs*? I thought being 11 *proactive* was a good thing.

Eva: I feel that I'm going to have to work twice as hard to earn some 12 *brownie point* to change his impression of me. I had better pay more attention to 13 *office etiquette*.

Alex: I'm going to have to think up ways to slow down without looking like I'm a 14 *slacker*.

Writing

CLB 5

Write a paragraph about what you could do to make a good impression on your first day at your job.

CLB 6

Write two paragraphs discussing how developing a working relationship with a mentor will help you transition into the company.

CLB 7

Write a two- or three-paragraph essay discussing why good working relationships are important in the workplace. How does this contribute to team building?

CLB 8

Research two or three Internet sites that have information on how to build positive workplace relationships. Describe and summarize what you learn in a four-paragraph essay. Remember to give an introduction, develop your main points, and finish with a conclusion.

Group work

Exercise A

In pairs or small groups, complete the crossword puzzle.

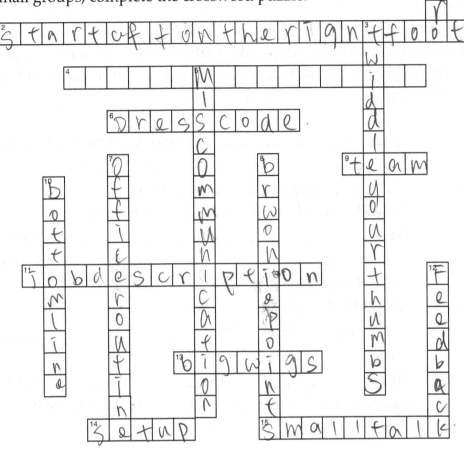

The completed crossword contains:
- 2 Across: start off on the right foot
- 4 Across: (blank)
- 6 Across: Dress code
- 9 Across: team
- 11 Across: job description
- 13 Across: bigwigs
- 14 Across: set up
- 15 Across: small talk
- 1 Down: proactive
- 3 Down: twiddle your thumbs
- 5 Down: miscommunication
- 7 Down: routine
- 8 Down: brownpoint
- 10 Down: bottom line
- 12 Down: feedback

Across

2. to begin well
4. a meeting between an employee and his manager, to discuss the quality of his work and to plan future tasks
6. a set of rules that an organization has about what employees must or must not wear
9. a group with shared goals and accountability
11. a written explanation of an employee's exact work responsibilities
13. company executives
14. make your work area functional and efficient: _____ your work station.
15. polite conversation about ordinary or unimportant subjects, especially at social occasions

Down

1. taking the initiative by being the first person to act in a situation: being _____ active
3. do nothing while you are waiting for something to happen
5. failure to communicate something well
7. the organization of someone's typical workday
8. do something to please your boss or gain recognition: earn _____
10. the important conclusion
12. advice, criticism, or information given to someone about how good or useful her work is

Exercise B

Discuss why it is important to participate in social activities in the workplace.

Exercise C

The present perfect and present perfect continuous verb tenses are often used when trying to engage people in small-talk. Decide whether the present perfect or present perfect continuous tense of each verb in parentheses should be used in the following dialogue.

Maria: I ₁ _____have' not seen ~~you~~_____ (to not see) you in a long time. How ₂ _____have_____ you _____to been_____ (to be)?

Jose: ₃ _____I've been_____ (to be) fine. I ₄ _____'ve been._____ (to work) out of the city for the last few months.

Maria: What ₅ _____'ve been_____ you _____doing_____ (to do)?

Jose: I ₆ _____have been selling_____ (to sell) computer software programs to medical institutions around the province.

Maria: No kidding! That's awesome, Jose.

Jose: But enough about me. What ₇ _____have_____ you _____been ~~to~~ doing_____ (to do)?

Maria: Recently, I ₈ _____have_____ just _____started_____ (to start) a new job as a pharmaceutical assistant in a department store. I love it!

Jose: That's wonderful, Maria.

Now with a partner, create your own small-talk conversation using the present perfect and present perfect continuous tenses.

On your own

Practise the present perfect and present perfect continuous tenses. There are many sites on the Internet that can provide information and practice tests.

Personal learning: practising English outside of the classroom

This past week I ... _____

Tomorrow I will try ... _____

My favourite new word is ... _____

By next class I will ... _____

Chapter 4

Projecting a Professional Image

Key Point Focus

- Stereotypes that may exist in the workplace
- Dressing well
- Personal grooming

First things first

Managing your personal traits may not be enough to present a professional image. You also belong to a social identity group that—whether justified or not—brings with it its own stereotyping. You can dress professionally, but how do you address the negative stereotypes that might exist about your social identity group? How might these undermine your image? For example, are you a working mother who might be perceived as being less committed to your profession and less loyal to your employer than a woman who has no children to take care of?

You must decide what you want your co-workers and superiors to say about you when you are not in the room. Use nonverbal cues such as your appearance and demeanour to establish a positive impression. Pay attention to your tone of voice and rate of speech. Demonstrate thoughtfulness in your daily work habits. Exhibit the qualities that you feel are most valued in the workplace.

Exercise A

Survey your peers to find out which qualities they feel are most valued in the workplace. Do you agree with these responses?

Qualities	Person 1	Person 2	Person 3	Person 4
Honesty				

Exercise B

An employer's impression of you can be made in the first few minutes of meeting you. Often this impression is reinforced by your personal appearance. Dressing for success in Canada is very important. Jim, the laboratory employee, is a good example. (*You're Hired...Now What?* p. 59) Despite the fact that he was an excellent worker, his sloppy and unkempt appearance prevented him from being promoted. His hair was dirty and uncombed, his shoes worn down, and he slouched a lot. He didn't look like potential management material. What should he have done to address this problem?

_____

_____

What do you believe personal grooming involves?

_____

Exercise C

Canadian Business Concept: Dress for the job you want, not for the job you have.

What does this expression mean? What does this mean to you?

_____

_____

Exercise D

Finding the right type of clothes to wear for your job requires familiarity with the stores in your area. Look at a number of store flyers and catalogues. With a partner, fill in the chart detailing the names of stores in your city, the types of stores they are, and the types of clothing they are likely to offer. Decide where you would most likely find the clothing that you would need for your profession.

Name of Store	Type of Store	Type of Clothing
The Bay	department store	sports wear, business wear, formal wear

Exercise E

Match each accessory or item of clothing with the correct picture.

briefcase	pump	suit
flip-flops	purse	sweater
jacket	raincoat	T-shirt
jeans	shirt	

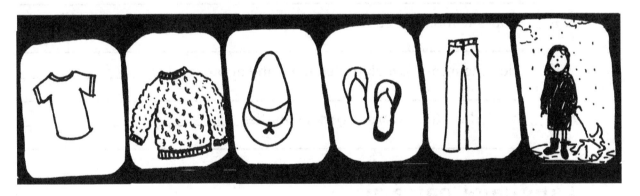

1. _____ 2. _____ 3. _____ 4. _____ 5. _____ 6. _____

7. _____ 8. _____ 9. _____ 10. _____ 11. _____

Buzzwords

Match each term or expression with its meaning and then use the expression in a sentence.

a)	feel like a million bucks	e)	look up-to-date
b)	five o'clock shadow	f)	out of style
c)	flats	g)	smart business
d)	little black dress	h)	spaghetti straps

1. __ day-old growth of beard on men _____

   _____

2. __ to walk and talk with confidence _____

   _____

3. __ to be smartly dressed in the latest styles _____

   _____

4. __ not aware of current fashion trends _____

   _____

5. __ thin straps on a party dress _____

   _____

6. __ shoes without raised heels _____

   _____

7. __ clothing meant to look professional and approachable ____

   _____

8. __ black dress to be worn to cocktail parties _____

   _____

Language patterns

Complete the definitions and then use each *dress* term in a sentence.

1. smartly dressed: *dressed appropriately for the occasion.* _____

   Becca was smartly dressed when she went for her interview. _____

2. overdressed: _____

   _____

3. dressed up: _____

   _____

4. dressed down: _____

   _____

5. dressed for success: _____

    _____

6. dressed to the nines: _____

    _____

Vocabulary

Discuss the following vocabulary with your classmates.

wardrobe	business casual	T-shirts
over accessorize	prints	wash and wear
trendy	fly-away hair	scents
pumps	hat hair	slogan

Dialogue

Use the vocabulary words from the previous section to complete the dialogue.

Andrea   Diwata

Andrea: Hello, Diwata. I was wondering if I could ask you for some advice.
Diwata: Certainly, Andrea. How can I help?
Andrea: My current $_1$ _____ is not suitable for my new job,
            and I was hoping you could help me figure out how to be well-dressed.
Diwata: Of course. (Laughing) I know how you feel. I wish someone had
            helped me dress properly when my first Canadian winter was
            upon me. I was not prepared and didn't have the right clothes or
            footwear for the snow.
            Anyway, choosing business clothing here means you should wear
            $_2$ _____ rather than stiletto heels on your feet.
            Also, be careful that you don't $_3$ _____
            with jewellery. The boss wants you to be smartly dressed, but not
            dressed to the nines.
Andrea: I didn't realize this.
Diwata: Watch how you wear your hair. I see you have it pulled back in a
            bun. That's great. The boss doesn't like $_4$ _____
            or $_5$ _____ which has been flattened by a hat.
Andrea: That is good to know.
Diwata: On Fridays, though, we have a dress-down day, so we can wear
            $_6$ _____ . This is our chance to wear casual
            pants and sweaters. Don't wear $_7$ _____ ,
            though. The boss doesn't like anything that has a $_8$ _____
            on it. I recommend something that is $_9$ _____
            so you don't have to iron it.

Andrea: Is it okay if I'm 10 _____? I like to keep up with the latest styles.

Diwata: Yes. You have to be careful that you remain relatively conservative in appearance, though. No loud 11 _____ or patterns to your clothes. The boss likes it clean and simple.

Andrea: What about perfume? Is it okay to wear it?

Diwata: No. There are a few people here who are very allergic, so the company has a no-12 _____ policy here. This is to stop really strong deodorant smells as well.

Andrea: Thank you so much, Diwata. This helps me a lot.

Writing

CLB 5

Write a paragraph describing what you would wear to an interview for a job in your chosen profession.

CLB 6

Write two paragraphs describing what you could wear on your first day of work at your job. Include the accessories that you could incorporate.

CLB 7

Write a three-paragraph description of yourself for a cover letter. Consider the characteristics that would contribute to your professional image.

CLB 8

Research two or three websites that deal with professional image. Describe and summarize the information in a four-paragraph essay. Remember to include an introduction, develop your main points, and finish with a conclusion.

Group work

Exercise A

Canadian Business Concept: If someone offers you a mint, take it!

What does this mean? What does this say about hygiene in Canada?

_____

How might this apply to Sanjay? (*You're Hired...Now What?* p.80) He was an employee of a software company who was well qualified for his job. However, people started to avoid him. Why? He showered every day, but often wore the same shirt to work for several days. What was his problem?

_____

Exercise B

In pairs, develop a dialogue between an employer and an employee about the employee's hygiene problem.

Exercise C

Work in pairs. What would you wear to the following company events?

1. cocktail party _____
2. dinner meeting _____
3. office holiday party _____
4. company picnic _____
5. dinner at your boss's house _____
6. business meeting with a client _____
7. sales call _____
8. (an event of your choice) _____

Exercise D

In groups, discuss your observations about Canadian dress codes in the workplace. How do these differ from those in other cultures you are familiar with?

Exercise E

The formality of the clothes you should wear will depend on the formality of the particular social situation you are in. This is also true for the form of English you should use. Decide which sentences are examples of formal (F) or informal (I) English. In which social situations would you most likely use them?

Sentence	Formal or Informal?	Social Situations
1. I don't know.	F I	
2. I dunno.	F I	
3. They've lived in Canada for many years.	F I	
4. They have lived in Canada for many years.	F I	
5. Have you finished your work?	F I	
6. Finished your work?	F I	
7. I have ten bucks.	F I	
8. I have ten dollars.	F I	

On your own

Research the typical dress code of your profession. What seem to be the essentials to be considered well-dressed for work?

On the Internet, look up examples of formal and informal English, and make a list of eight to ten of the examples. Decide on which types of occasions you would use each one.

Personal learning: practising English outside of the classroom

This past week I ... _____

Tomorrow I will try ... _____

My favourite new word is ... _____

By next class I will ... _____

Chapter 5

Actions Speak Louder Than Words

Key Point Focus

- Non-verbal messages in different cultures
- Body language as a key to understanding unspoken workplace expectations

First things first

People from every culture have their own ways of communicating without words. Non-verbal communication can include body and eye movements, gestures, facial expressions, use of physical space, postures, touch, smell, and silence. Often, all of these things are grouped together and called body language.

Canadians have "space bubbles." These are measurable amounts of physical space that people need around them in order to feel comfortable. People will attempt to step back or move away if someone comes into their intimate space. Most Canadians feel uncomfortable if someone stands closer than 45 centimetres from them, with the exception of close friends or family members. Each culture has its own space comfort zone.

In some cultures, it is very acceptable to touch other people when greeting or talking. In North America, touch involves the intimate space and only occurs with the initial greeting handshake. After the firm handshake, people will generally take a step back to get out of the other person's intimate zone.

Watch people as they enter an elevator. Where do they stand? How close do they stand to each other? What do they look at? Do they talk to each other? Do they touch each other? Which way do they face? Watch people as they stand in line at a grocery store. How close do they stand to each other? Where do they look? Do they talk to each other? Watch people as they sit together and talk in coffee shops. What do you observe?

Smell can communicate messages of attraction, memory, and repulsion. Smell sends a very powerful message and remains in the memory long after the person or thing that caused the smell is gone. Most westerners respond negatively to what they would consider bad smells. These include perspiration, body odour, bad breath, and unwashed clothing. Mint, pine, fruits, and flowers are considered acceptable smells. However, many buildings have fragrance-free zones where perfume is not to be worn because of the increasing number of people with allergies to strong scent.

Observing non-verbal communication is a positive first step toward trying to understand the unspoken expectations of the workplace. A genuine smile, appropriate eye contact, and a firm handshake are essential elements of creating a positive impression.

Exercise A

Underline any vocabulary from the First things first section that you do not know. Work with a partner to compare lists. Help each other fill in the definitions for the new vocabulary. Add these words to your personal vocabulary notebook.

Exercise B

1. Read First things first again and draw a circle around four words that you think are key to understanding the article.
2. In small groups, compare the key words you identified. Try to think of other phrases or words that have a similar meaning. Add the keywords and their synonyms to the table.

smell			
scent			
odour			

Buzzwords

comfort zone: area in which you feel confident and comfortable (referring to ideas or physical space)

face-to-face: (communicating) in person, not by email or telephone

hands-on: having personal involvement in a task

heartfelt: genuine feelings

pay lip service: pretend or say that you will do something but not really do it

status quo: the situation as it usually is

walk the talk: do what you say is important, don't just talk about it

Exercise A

Complete each sentence with a buzzword from the list above.

1. We need a ____*face to face*____ meeting to sort out our plans. Email is just not helping us right now.
2. I have difficulty with that type of party. It is out of my ____*comfort zone*____.
3. People say they are concerned about the environment. But I wish they would ____*walk the talk*____ and put their old newspapers in the recycle bin.
4. They ____*pay lip service*____ to saving energy, but leave all the lights on when they are not in a room.
5. I prefer a ____*hands-on*____ approach. I would like to actually do something to help out.
6. What is the ____*status quo*____ ? How do things usually work around here?
7. He really means what he says. That was a ____*heartfelt*____ message.

Exercise B

In pairs, compare your answers. Create an additional sentence for each buzzword.

Language patterns

1. Review the phrasal verbs in the chart on the following page. If you already know the meaning, put a checkmark (✓) beside the definition. If you have never seen the word *hand* used like that before, put an X beside that definition.
2. Complete the chart.
3. In pairs, compare your answers. Use your drawings to explain the different uses of *hand* to each other.

Phrasal Verb	Hand out	Hand over	Hand down	Hand down	Hand in
Definition	To give something to each person in a group	To give control or responsibility to another person	To leave something to a younger person	To announce an official decision	To give something to someone in an official position
Example sentence	Please hand out these papers to the class	The parents are going to hand over control of the business to their children	The family recipes have been handed down from parent to child	The court will hand down a decision about the new law	He is waiting until his birthday to hand in his official retirement notice
Your own example sentence	Garld you please help me To hand out there	sb. need to hand out control of the leadship to other	The necklace have been handed down from my grand mother to me	The company will hand down a decision abou new program	A offer has been handed in from the university
A drawing to help you remember how to use this phrasal verb	photoc to our classmates out = give	over = end	down = perso younger	program	in = offer

Use a phrasal verbs dictionary to look up other definitions for each of these patterns. Create a chart in your notebook similar to the one above to help you remember the new definitions.

Vocabulary

attraction	⌄gesture	perspiration
✓acceptable	⌄intimate	✓zone
fragrance	✓personal	✓observe
⌄posture	✓initial	✓genuine
scent	memory	repulsion

1. Review the vocabulary words above. If you know the meaning of a word, put a checkmark (✓) next to it. If you think you might know what it means, put a question mark (?) next to it, and write what you think the word means. If you have never seen the word before, put an X next to it.

2. In pairs, compare lists. Write example sentences for the words with a checkmark or question mark.

3. Look up the words that are totally unknown to both of you, and add these words to your vocabulary notebook.

Dialogue

Sami   Cam

The dialogue below includes some idiomatic language. Translate it into standard English.

	Idiomatic English	Standard English
Sami	Hi. I'm glad we are finally having this face-to-face. I need to give you a heads-up about tomorrow's team meeting.	*Hi. I'm glad we are finally able to talk in person. I need to give you some advance warning about tomorrow's team meeting.*
Cam	Oh. What's up?	*Oh. What is happening?*
Sami	Well, the bottom line is that it is really a surprise birthday party for Mia.	
Cam	That's nice.	
Sami	The first few agenda items will be status quo and then Raul is going to hand out some papers to everyone except Mia. They are song sheets with new words to "Happy Birthday." We are all going to sing a few lines.	
Cam	Oh my. Singing is out of my comfort zone. I sound terrible.	
Sami	Well, just move your lips.	
Cam	Okay. I will pay lip service to the song. But my good wishes for her birthday will be heartfelt.	
Sami	We are also handing around a birthday card at coffee break tomorrow. Make sure you sign it.	
Cam	Thanks so much for the heads-up. See you tomorrow.	

Exercise A

In pairs, practise the original dialogue (with idioms). Then write your own dialogue about a behaviour you have observed in the workplace. Follow the example above and use two columns—one for idiomatic English and one for standard English. Try to use one idiom in each sentence.

Exercise B

Use the vocabulary to create a role play about body language in Canada.

Writing

Idioms are not generally used in formal written business communication. However, they are widely used in face-to-face verbal messages, speeches, and presentations.

The following task is to write an informal letter to a friend. Use two idioms and two vocabulary words from this chapter in your letter.

CLB 5

Write a 150-word letter explaining your understanding of the saying *Actions speak louder than words*.

CLB 6

Write a 200-word letter explaining your understanding of the saying *Actions speak louder than words*.

CLB 7

Write a 250-word letter explaining your understanding of the saying *Actions speak louder than words*.

CLB 8

Write a 400-word letter to explain a minor confusion that resulted from a non-verbal misunderstanding between you and another colleague at work. Describe the situation. Use the saying *Actions speak louder than words* to help explain the way you resolved the interaction.

Group work

Exercise A

As you complete the steps below, write your findings in the chart.

1. Work with a partner. Stand up. Spread your arms out in front of you to your full arm length. Then extend them out to your sides. This is your personal "space bubble."
2. Face your partner. Create personal space bubbles. Take a ruler and measure the distance between your feet and your partner's feet. It should be a minimum of 45 centimetres.

3. Take one step backward. Measure the distance again. Record your distance. This is your social zone.

4. Imagine that you have to give a presentation to your class. Ask your partner to step backward until you feel that he or she is standing at a comfortable distance from you—this should be the distance at which your closest audience members would be during your presentation. Measure the distance. This is your public zone.

5. How close can someone stand to you before you feel uncomfortable? Experiment with your partner. Ask him or her to walk toward you. When your partner is as close as you feel comfortable with, say "stop." Measure the distance. This is the limit of your personal comfort zone. This may be different for each individual, as it depends on culture and personality.

Zone	Amount of Space	When Does This Apply?	My Own Comfort Zones
Intimate	Less than 45 cm (18 inches)	Interacting with family or close friends	
Personal	45 cm to 120 cm (18 inches to 4 feet)	Giving instructions or working with others	
Social	120 cm to 3.5 m (4 to 12 feet)	Most business situations, such as meetings or discussions	
Public	More than 3.5 m (12 feet)	Giving a speech	

Exercise B

In small groups, discuss the social distance differences in various cultures.

Exercise C

In small groups, discuss and complete the chart below.

Are there any other areas of non-verbal communication in which you have noticed differences between your culture and Canada? Discuss these with your group.

Non-verbal Communication Area	What I Have Observed in Canada	What Is Traditional and Comfortable for Me
Hand gestures		
Touching		
Facial gestures		
Smells		
Eye contact		

On your own

At your local public library, look for books on interpersonal communication skills. What information about non-verbal communication do these offer?

Do an online search for *Non-verbal communication*. Add the word *Canadian* for your next search. Add the word *Western* for another search. Do these searches bring up different results? Do you notice any patterns?

Take notes on your findings and share your information with the class.

Personal learning: practising English outside of the classroom

I will add these buzzwords to my vocabulary notebook: _____

I need to practise ... _____

The most important thing I have learned about non-verbal communication is ...

_____

By next class I will ... _____

Business Talk on the Job

Key Point Focus

- Canadian communication: direct but polite
- Buzzwords, idioms, and phrasal verbs
- Choosing your words carefully

First things first

Understanding verbal communication can be a complex process. There are many things that can both help and hinder clear communication. The cultures in which people grow up have a huge influence on their communication styles. Even within the same culture, there can be differences in accents and word meaning.

Although people talk about a Canadian way of communicating, Canadians across the country have slightly different accents and may use slightly different sets of buzzwords and idioms. Place of residence, cultural background, and educational achievements are important factors in influencing how people talk.

Canadians use a direct style of communication. Communication is considered effective when there is a clear exchange of both information and understanding. Basically, this means that the message that one person intended to send is the actual message that the other person receives. This clarity is a goal: yes means yes. However, Canadians also value polite conversation. *Please, thank you, pardon me,* and *excuse me* are words and phrases that are part of daily conversation.

People who are new to Canada often have difficulty with buzzwords and idioms. It is as if Canadians are speaking a language other than English. Many conversations can be composed entirely of idioms. If you listen and hear words and phrases that do not make any sense, you are probably hearing idioms and phrasal verbs. Write them down. Look them up. Ask people about them. An understanding of these terms is one of the keys that will help you understand English in Canada.

Exercise A

Underline any vocabulary words from First things first that you do not know. Work with a partner to compare lists. Help each other fill in the definitions for the new vocabulary words. Add these words to your personal vocabulary notebook.

Exercise B

Polite Conversations

Below are a few polite expressions. What other ones have you heard? Under what circumstances would you use these expressions? Work in a small group to share your observations and complete the chart.

Category	Expressions	Situation: When would you use these expressions? Give an example.
Greeting	• Hello, I'm Maria from Maple Company. • Nice to meet you. • It was a pleasure meeting you.	
Time	• Do you have a moment? • I'll just be a moment. • I'll just be a minute. • Is this a convenient time for you? • Are you busy just now? • Can you spare a moment?	
Apologizing	• I'm sorry. • Excuse me. • Could you please excuse me for a moment?	
Interrupting	• May I jump in for a moment? • Excuse me, but I wonder if ...? • Sorry for the interruption, but ... • Pardon me, but could I ...?	
Customer Service	• How can I help you? • May I help you? • Can I be of help? • Is there anything I could help you with?	
Saying Yes	• Sure. • No problem. • Of course. • Yes, that will be fine. • Thank you. That will be great. • Yes. That will work.	
Saying No	• No thank you. • Thank you for thinking of me, but no thanks. • Not at the moment, thank you. • Thanks. But I am not interested.	
What other expressions have you heard?		

Buzzwords

Exercise A

Match each idiom with its meaning.

1.	hog the floor ___	a)	what is happening?
2.	get to the point ___	b)	express in a simple clear way without extra information or feelings
3.	win-win strategy ___	c)	expressed in a clear brief way
4.	in a nutshell ___	d)	speak at a public meeting for a long time without stopping
5.	what's up? ___	e)	put effort and enthusiasm into something that is difficult
6.	sink one's teeth into ___	f)	plan in which everybody involved achieves success
7.	brain-dead ___	g)	unable to think

Exercise B

Fill in the blanks with the correct buzzwords from above.

1.   We are in a hurry so I'll give you the latest news ———————————— .
2.   I haven't seen you all week. ————————————?
3.   I will ———————————— , the news is very good.
4.   I feel like I need a new and difficult project to ———————————— .

In pairs, compare your answers. Create sentences for the idioms that have not yet been used in the sentences above.

Language patterns

Look up the word *have* in a phrasal verbs dictionary.

Create your own sentences about workplace communication using the following expressions. Share your results with a partner. Are there any similarities?

Have Term	Your Sentence
have difficulty	*Some people have difficulty communicating politely yet clearly.*
have an opportunity	
have trouble	
have a plan	
have an argument	
have an idea	
have an interest	

Vocabulary

clarity	consider	influence
complex	exchange	residence
compose	hinder	sense

Complete these sentences and compare your answers with a partner. Use your dictionary if you are unsure of the meaning of any of the words.

1. When I go to work I have to consider … _____
2. I don't want to hinder … _____
3. English can be a complex … _____
4. I don't want to influence you, but … _____
5. My principal residence is … _____
6. My best achievement … _____
7. I would like to exchange … _____
8. Just for clarity … _____
9. I need to compose … _____
10. At least he had enough sense to … _____

Dialogue

Marco	Kim

		Idiomatic English	Standard English
Marco		Hi Kim. Do you have a minute?	Hi Kim. Are you busy?
Kim		Sure Marco. What's up?	I am not busy right now Marco. What do you need (or want)?
Marco		Well, I have to start a new group project and I wanted to run a few concerns by you.	Well, I have started a new group project and I wanted to discuss a few of my concerns with you.
Kim		All right. Shoot.	All right. Tell me about them.
Marco		In a nutshell, I am concerned about the group. They seem brain-dead.	I will summarize in a clear and brief way. The group seems unable to think and respond appropriately to the project.
Kim		Oh! That's strong language. Did you say that to them?	Oh! Those are words that would make people feel upset and attacked. Did you say that to them?
Marco		No. Of course not. That would not be a win-win strategy. You know the ropes around here. What do you think I could do to help them?	No. Of course not .That would not be the best way to help everyone involved to achieve success. You know how to do things correctly around here. What do you think I could do to help them?
Kim		Um, let me think about this and I'll get back to you.	I need to think about this for a while and will share my ideas with you later.
Marco		Thanks. That would be great.	Thanks. That would be great.

Exercise A

In pairs, practise the original dialogue (with idioms). Then write your own dialogue about a current news event. Follow the example and use two columns—one for idiomatic English and one for standard English. Try to use one idiom in each sentence.

Exercise B

In groups of four, role play the following situation. Use the buzzwords and vocabulary words from this chapter.

You are all members of the Health and Safety Committee for your organization. Each group member is to prepare an explanation about the need for new and more detailed heath and safety guidelines. Discuss which guidelines would be most helpful. How should these guidelines be communicated to the other employees?

Writing

CLB 5 and CLB 6

Write an email expressing thanks in response to an invitation to join the Social Committee at your company.

CLB 7

Write an email expressing thanks in response to an invitation to join the Social Committee at your company. Clarify the date and location of the upcoming meeting.

CLB 8

Write an email expressing thanks in response to an invitation to join the Social Committee at your company. Clarify the date and location of the upcoming meeting. Include reassurance that you will be able to be an active member of the committee.

Group work

Exercise A

If you say ...	Yes	No	Maybe
It can mean ...	I agree	I disagree	Perhaps
	I understand	I don't understand	I'm not sure
	I will do it	I won't do it	Let me think about this
	I will follow your directions	I will not follow your directions	I cannot make a promise
	I can do it	I can't do it	Possibly
	You are right	I am not able to do it	*Uncertain*
	I did	You are wrong	
	Certainly	I did not	
	Affirmative	I can't	
		I don't think so	
		Negative	

In pairs, ask each other non-personal work-related questions. You should respond to each question with a direct but polite reply.

For example,

"Did you go to the meeting last week?"   "No, I didn't."

"Would you be able to stay late tonight to help the Health and Safety Committee?"   "No. I'm sorry. I can't tonight."

Exercise B

1. Work with a partner. Use the chart from Exercise A to give affirmative, negative, and uncertain answers to these questions:

    Do you think it will rain tomorrow?   Do you know how to change the toner in the copier?

    Are you available for overtime work?

    Do you know how to fix the coffee maker?   Would you be able to help with the cleanup?

2. Create some general questions about employment in your province or territory. Take turns using a variety of direct responses.

Exercise C

Give instructions to your partner about how to do something, such as make a paper airplane, cook rice, find an office supply store, or purchase work boots. Use the sentences in the box to help with your answers.

Clarifying Information
1. I am not sure if I understood exactly what you would like. Could you please repeat that? **4.** What should I do after that?

1. I am not sure if I understood exactly what you would like. Could you please repeat that?

2. So, first I _____ and then I _____ . Is that correct?

3. Is there anything else that I should know before I start?

4. What should I do after that?

5. Excuse me; I'm still unclear about _____ _____

6. Could you explain that in a little more detail, please?

7. Could you tell me a little more about _____ ?

Exercise D

Emotive language can start arguments and make people upset. Emotive language creates an emotional response. Saying the right thing at the right time in the right way is sometimes very hard. A careful choice of words may be the difference between having a conversation and starting an argument. Some words carry positive emotions, others negative or neutral. Neutral words are considered the best choice for emails.

In small groups, answer the following questions.

1. What are some of the communication difficulties that people have with email? _____

_____

2. Are there special words in your culture that create an emotional response?

_____

3. Complete the chart.

Positive Words	Negative Words	Neutral Words
thrifty	cheap	economical
	old-fashioned	
	loud	
	chatterbox	

What other words could cause an emotional reaction? Add them to the chart.

4. Could some positive words be also considered neutral words? Give examples.

_____

On your own
Exercise B

1. Listen carefully when people speak to you at meetings, in the cafeteria, at the grocery store, and at coffee shops. Write down the phrases you don't understand in your notebook. Look them up in either a phrasal verbs dictionary or an idioms dictionary. If you cannot find the phrases in the dictionary, bring the list to class and ask your classmates and instructors about the meanings.

2. Go to the public library and ask the librarian to suggest a magazine or journal about working in Canada. Read an article. Read it a second time, and write down any unfamiliar words. Can you guess at their meaning? Look up the words.

3. Do an online search for the topic *How to deal with difficult people*. Take notes. Bring your notes to the next class.

4. Watch a sitcom (situation comedy) or a drama on TV. Write down the phrases that you did not understand. Bring the list to class.

5. Listen to a talk program on the radio. Write down unfamiliar phrases. Add them to your collection.

Personal learning: practising English outside of the classroom

I have learned about … _____

My favourite new word is … _____

By next class I will … _____

Business Talk on the Job

Key Point Focus
- Listening skills as a part of effective communication
- Giving and receiving feedback

First things first

Listening and feedback skills are essential components of workplace communication. Effective listening helps to minimize the risk of misunderstanding, and skilful feedback helps to clarify messages.

Listening requires paying careful attention to the speaker. What really happens when you listen? Do you hear everything someone says? Do you listen only to the words and the details? Or do you try to understand the emotions and feelings that accompany the facts? Do you always accurately remember everything you have heard? Does your mind wander if you do not find a speaker interesting? Answering these questions for yourself will begin to provide you with some understanding of your own listening habits.

Feedback can be both given and taken. Feedback, in workplace settings, is a term that is used to refer to information that is given or solicited in response to communication, a product, or a person's performance of a task.

In a workplace, the supervisor, leader, manager, or human resources (HR) department may give feedback to an employee about the quality of his or her work. Businesses often send out customer surveys to solicit feedback about their products and services. Co-workers may ask for or offer feedback to one another about work concerns.

Giving feedback that is helpful and appropriate is another effective communication skill. Mastering this skill is all about what you say and how you say it.

Exercise A

In pairs, discuss which of the following statements support the ideas about listening and feedback presented in the First things first section. Circle your answers.

1. Listening is a skill.
2. Effective communication requires listening skills.
3. People pay attention to everything they hear.
4. Feedback can either be positive or negative.
5. Many cultures have similar expectations about listening and feedback.

Exercise B

In small groups, share your ideas about the statements above. What are your opinions about listening and feedback?

Use the following expressions as a starting point for your feedback responses:

- From my experience, I have found that …
- From my point of view, I think …
- To be honest with you, I feel …
- If you ask me, listening ought to …
- Actually, I think that many cultures have …

Exercise C

Feedback tips: keeping it professional

Here are a few feedback suggestions. Work with a partner to add more feedback tips to each heading.

Giving Feedback			Getting Feedback
Be sure to ...	Document	Think	Be sure to ...
• present the facts • be accurate • use examples to explain • not use blame	• keep a paper trail of emails and letters • keep a journal with meeting dates	• about what you want to say • about how you want to say it • about where and when you want to give or receive feedback	• be clear about the kind of feedback you would like • listen calmly • try to understand • ask for clarification • say thank you
Add your own ideas			
• • • • •	• • • • •	• • • • •	• • • • •

Buzzwords

1. The chart below contains some buzzwords and their meanings. Create a sentence using each expression.

Buzzword	Meaning	Example Sentence
catch on	understand something / realize the truth	*It took a long time for them to catch on to the fact that the diamond was a fake.*
pay attention	listen carefully	
point of view	opinion / one way of looking at or judging something	
paper trail	collected sequence of letters, emails, or documents that verify information	
left in the dark	having no information about something	
on the ball	aware of what is happening and able to react or deal with it quickly	
think outside the box	think about something or how to do something in a new or creative way	

For more complete definitions, refer to a phrasal verbs dictionary or an idioms dictionary.

2. Choose a buzzword from the chart above to complete each of these sentences.
   a) I have an important announcement.
      Could you please _____ ?
   b) The team will soon_____ to the idea that the meetings are the best place to share information.
   c) Things can happen so quickly that we need someone in that security position who is really_____ .
   d) The company is looking for bright, creative people who can _____ .
   e) The workers were _____ about the plans to shut down the company over the summer.
   f) Remember to create a _____ if you want to provide accurate documented feedback about your concerns.
   g) They have a right to their _____ . However, I feel there are other opinions that also need to be considered.

Language patterns

Exercise A

In pairs, discuss the advantages and disadvantages of the different types of feedback.

Description of Feedback	Advantages	Disadvantages
Positive: focusing on things that are good about a situation		
Negative: focusing on things that are bad or harmful		
Constructive: having a useful effect		
Supportive: giving help and encouragement		
Critical: providing careful judgments about good and bad qualities of something		
Immediate: done without delay		
Delayed: done with delay		
Specific: detailed and exact		
Vague: not clear and without enough information		
Realistic: detailing changes that are possible to achieve, appropriate, and sensible		

Which types of feedback would you prefer to give? Which types of feedback would you prefer to receive? Why? Discuss your point of view with your partner.

Exercise B

Write one sentence about each type of feedback.

1. *Giving positive feedback is an enjoyable task as it is something that helps to encourage and motivate people.*
2. *Giving negative feedback is ...*
3. _____
4. _____
5. _____
6. _____
7. _____
8. _____
9. _____
10. _____

Exercise C

In small groups, discuss and answer the following questions.

Receiving feedback involves listening to another person. What can get in the way of our ability to listen? What are the essential considerations involved in giving appropriate feedback? In what ways can people improve their listening skills?

Vocabulary

appropriate	feedback	provide
component	habit	refer
constructive	minimize	response
essential	performance	solicit

Complete these sentences using the vocabulary words above, then compare your answers with a partner.

1. To minimize misunderstanding, we could … _____
2. I have a habit of … _____
3. Helpful feedback is … _____

4. It is essential to … _____

5. Please provide a … _____

6. An appropriate response to an emergency is to … _____

7. Please refer to a dictionary for … _____

8. A constructive way to solve the problem of the bad coffee is to …

_____

9. To solicit feedback about my project, I should … _____

Write a paragraph using six of the vocabulary words to describe your listening and feedback skills.

Dialogue

| Tran | Kim |

Tran: I hope I haven't done anything to offend you.

Kim: What do you mean?

Tran: I sent an email to you last week and I haven't heard back from you.

Kim: I'm not sure what you are referring to.

Tran: I sent you an email last Friday asking if you could give me some feedback on my ideas for the meeting.

Kim: Oh! I am so sorry. I got sick at lunch time on Thursday and ended up in emergency. This is my first day back. I'm not on the ball yet.

Tran: Oh my. That's too bad. I didn't hear about that. How are you feeling now?

Kim: I'm fine. A little tired, but fine. Referring back to your email questions, I have a moment right now if you have time to talk.

Tran: I would really appreciate hearing your point of view on the essential components. It shouldn't take long. Thanks so much. I really appreciate this.

Kim: No problem.

Exercise A

1.   Work with a partner to practise the dialogue.
2.   Write a new dialogue in which someone requests feedback; incorporate a new problem into your dialogue. Use as many buzzwords and vocabulary words as you can.
3.   Write a third dialogue in which someone offers another person feedback on a work concern.

Exercise B

1. In a small group, create a list of workplace topics that could require feedback.

• work quality	•
• deadlines	•
• new ideas	•
•	•
•	•

2. With your group, role play situations in which you request and give feedback about these topics.

Writing

CLB 5

Create guidelines for giving feedback in the workplace. Include three things people could do to give helpful feedback.

CLB 6

Create guidelines for giving feedback in the workplace. Include five steps in your instructions.

CLB 7

Create procedural guidelines for giving feedback in the workplace. Include seven steps in your instructions.

CLB 8

Create procedural guidelines for giving feedback in the workplace. Include ten steps in your instructions.

Group work

Exercise A

Read the following comments. Rate each comment as *helpful* or *not helpful*. Compare your opinions with your group.

Feedback Comments	Helpful	Not Helpful
You must be crazy. I can't do that.		
It would be helpful if just one person talked at a time.		
That is an interesting idea, and here is another way we could think about it.		
That is very interesting. I never thought about it from that point of view.		
That was a stupid thing to do. You should have known better. That was a complete waste of time.		
I would really appreciate your feedback on this.		

On your own

1. Research the topic *Giving and receiving feedback* online. Take notes. Make a list of four ideas you consider important and take the list to your next class to discuss with your classmates.
2. Listen to a radio program that invites people to call in with their ideas. What kinds of feedback do you hear? Is it specific, accurate, and constructive?

Personal learning: practising English outside of the classroom

This past week I ... _____

Tomorrow I will give positive feedback to ... _____

My workplace English is improving because ... _____

By next class I will ... _____

I still need help with ... _____

Chapter 7

Telephone Tips

Key Point Focus

- Telephone etiquette
- Leaving clear messages
- Common telephone phrases

First things first

Each time you answer the phone at work you are representing your organization. Creating a positive impression is important. The caller will form an impression of both you and your organization by the way in which you answer the phone. Being able to answer the phone professionally and being able to respond clearly and politely is essential. If you record an outgoing voicemail message, it should be detailed yet brief and provide your contact information.

Phone conversations differ from face-to-face conversations because you cannot see the person with whom you are talking. You do not have the opportunity to see his or her facial expressions or body language. For this reason, it is necessary to be extra polite during a phone conversation. To show courtesy and respect, avoid interrupting your caller. Let the other person finish speaking before you respond.

You may occasionally need to apologize and ask for something to be repeated to confirm that you have all the necessary information. A good strategy to use to reduce the need for this is to make notes while on the phone. This will help you to remember the key points that were discussed.

Professional telephone skills involve clarity, etiquette, and lots of practice.

Exercise A

Telephone skills self-assessment

Use this short assessment to help you identify your telephone challenges.

Scoring
1 = Never 2 = Seldom 3 = Sometimes 4 = Almost always 5 = Always

I am comfortable when I answer the phone.	1	2	3	4	5
I can greet callers professionally.	1	2	3	4	5
I am able to transfer calls.	1	2	3	4	5
I give clear messages.	1	2	3	4	5
I close calls politely.	1	2	3	4	5
I wait until the caller also says goodbye before I hang up.	1	2	3	4	5

Look at your scores. Any items that you marked as 4 or lower are opportunities to improve your telephone skills.

Work with a partner to create a list of guidelines to help improve telephone skills.

Exercise B

In pairs, review the commonly used telephone phrases below, and translate each one into your native language.

What other phrases have you heard? Identify other commonly used telephone phrases and add them to the chart.

Category	Phrase	Translation into Your Language
Greeting	Hello. This is _____ from _____ company. May I please speak with _____?	
Apology	I'm afraid she's unavailable to take your call right now. I'm sorry, he's on another line. Would you like to leave a message on her voicemail?	
Asking to repeat	I'm sorry, I didn't catch that. Excuse me, would you mind repeating that?	
Ending the call	Thank you for that information. I will _____. Goodbye. Thanks so much. Goodbye.. Thank you for calling.	
Other situations		

Buzzwords

call you back	hold	run through
cut off	hold a moment	transfer
do's and don'ts	not available	voicemail
go over	put you through	wrong number
have a moment		

Complete each sentence by using one of the words or phrases above. Use each phrase only once.

1. She's unavailable today. Would you like me to _____ to her voicemail?
2. Please _____ while I look up that number for you.
3. I'm afraid Mr. Green is _____ at the moment.
4. Would you like to leave a message on his _____?
5. I would like to _____ the work schedule with you.
6. Hello. This is Anne from X Company. Do you _____ to talk about the project?
7. Sorry for the delay. I will _____ you now.
8. We have a new phone system. If you accidentally get _____, I will call you back.
9. When is a good time to _____?
10. I'm sorry, but you have the _____.

Language patterns

Polite questions: making requests

In Chapter 1, you used *could* and *would* to ask for help. These words are also used to show courtesy on the phone. Using *could you* or *would you* at the beginning of a sentence helps to make a request sound polite.

Complete the following sentences.

Could I *take a message?*
Could I *tell her who is calling?*
Could I _____?
Could you please *transfer me to his voicemail?*
Could you please send _____?
Could you _____?
Could you please provide me with _____?

Would you like *to leave a message?*

Would you like *to be put through to her voicemail?*

Would you like ———————————————— ?

Would you please ———————————————— ?

Vocabulary

annoy	courtesy	frustrating
apologize	deadline	impression
approximately	delay	interrupt
convenient	disconnected	summarize
courteous	discreet	

Using six of the vocabulary words, write a paragraph that describes a recent telephone conversation. In small groups, read your paragraphs to each other. Look up any vocabulary words that were not used in any of your paragraphs.

Dialogue

Mia	Guy

Mia: Hello, this is Mia Gill from ———————————— . May I speak to Rick Nairn, please?

Guy: Hello. I'm sorry, Mr. Nairn is not in the building today. May I take a message, or would you like to be transferred to his voicemail?

Mia: Which method will be the fastest way to reach him? I have a deadline that I am trying to meet.

Guy: Well, he always checks his voicemail at the end of each day, whether he is in the building or not. Voicemail would be the most convenient way to make sure he gets your message today.

Mia: Thanks. Please transfer me to his voicemail then.

Guy: Certainly.

Mia: Thanks again. Goodbye.

Guy: I will transfer you now. Goodbye.

Exercise A

Work with a partner to create dialogues for the situations below. How would the dialogue change?

New situations
- Rick Nairn is available.
- Rick Nairn is in a meeting.
- Your call went directly to Rick's voicemail.

Exercise B

Fill in the blanks in the chart below. Then work with a partner to create your own telephone dialogue. Remember to greet, state the reason for your call, confirm information, and end the call politely.

Parts of a Call	Dialogue
Beginning	Do you have a moment to talk? I just need five minutes to fill you in on _____ . I wanted to apologize for the _____ . I am very sorry it took so long. I wanted to thank you for the _____ . It was very helpful.
Clarification of Availability	I understand that you are busy just now. When would be a convenient time for me to call you back? Would _____ be a good time to call you back? It sounds like you are very busy. Should I call back _____ ? Is this a convenient time to talk with you about _____ ?
Clarification of Reason for Call	I wanted to ask you about _____ . I would like to tell you about _____ . I wonder if you could tell me more about _____ . Just to let you know, on Friday _____ . That is really interesting. Thanks for telling me about_____ . I can understand how _____ it is when something is late.
Confirmation of Information	Just to confirm your email address, could you please give it to me again? I would like to confirm the correct spelling of your name. Is that A as in apple? And _____ as in _____ ? Could you spell that, please? So, in summary, we will _____ and you will _____ .
Topic of Your Own Choosing	

Writing

Look in your local phone book. Find the 1-800 numbers for Government of Canada offices in the blue pages of the phone book. Call the number for one of the offices after business hours to hear the information message. You could also look up and call the number for Environment Canada's weather report and take notes about the weather forecast.

CLB 5

Take notes based on the message you hear.

CLB 6

Take notes based on the message you hear. In your notes, include the name of the department and the office hours.

CLB 7

Take notes based on the message you hear. What is the name of the department, and when is the office open? Where else does the message suggest you look for information?

CLB 8

Take notes based on the message you hear. What is the name of the department, and when is the office open? Where else does the message suggest you look for information? What is the email address?

Group work

Exercise A

Work in groups of three. Each group member has a role:
- Person 1 is the caller.
- Person 2 is the receiver of the call.
- Person 3 is the observer who will listen and give feedback and suggestions to Person 1 and Person 2 at the end of the call.

Rotate roles after each conversation so that each person has an opportunity to try each role.

Role play the following telephone situations:
- Confirming a dental appointment
- Checking the train schedule
- Making a car rental reservation
- Clarifying the agenda for a meeting
- Changing a meeting location and giving new directions
- Cancelling an order for a telephone service

Exercise B

Select your best telephone interaction from Exercise A and record it. Play the recording to the class. Ask for suggestions and comments.

Exercise C

Has your employer explained the company's telephone protocol? What is appropriate cellphone etiquette? Share your understanding of the company's expectations and your real-life experiences with your group.

Exercise D

Write a message for your home answering machine. With your group, discuss what information should be included and what should not be included.

On your own

Call some local businesses and community service centres after business hours. Take notes based on their voicemail messages. Did the messages provide basic details about the organizations?

Look up *Voicemail etiquette* and *Telephone etiquette tips* online, and try to find some useful suggestions. Select information from Canada first.

Personal learning: practising English outside of the classroom

This past week I ... _____

Tomorrow I will try to _____ while I am on the phone.

Today in class I learned ... _____

By next class I will have _____ more entries in my telephone phrase list. (See page 56.)

Chapter 8

Business Writing That Gets Results

Key Point Focus

- Memos and emails
- Avoiding business speak
- Best practices for using email in the workplace

First things first

The importance of writing clearly and professionally cannot be overstated. It is particularly crucial that your grammar be accurate and error-free. One aspect which seems to confuse many speakers of English as a second language concerns the use of the apostrophe. Probably the best rule to follow to simplify problems is to restrict its use to the possessive (for example, the boy's hat, people's concerns) and to replacing missing letters in words (I'm, we're). We tend not to use the apostrophe for pluralized abbreviations such as CDs or MPs. Apostrophes are also not used in numbers such as 1980s and over-50s.

Something else that you need to think about when writing your business correspondence concerns the type of font style you use. Sans serif fonts such as Arial and Tahoma give your message a modern image, but they take longer to read. Serif fonts such as Times New Roman give a less modern image, but they have a horizontal flow which helps with readability and reading comfort. Regardless of the style you choose, avoid the non-standard fonts. They may look innovative, but they are much more difficult to read.

> Arial
>
> Tahoma
>
> Times New Roman

Exercise A

Work in pairs. Decide whether the apostrophe in each sentence has been used correctly or not.

Sentence	Apostrophe used correctly?
1. The womens' decisions have been tabulated.	Yes / No
2. The team played it's part.	Yes / No
3. It's been a long day.	Yes / No
4. Dave painted all of the rowboat's.	Yes / No
5. Sheila's not going to meet us for lunch.	Yes / No
6. By week's end, we were tired.	Yes / No

Exercise B

Look at the formal business letter on the following page. Correct the mistakes in grammar, spelling, punctuation, and protocol. Information may have to be moved around.

Buzzwords

Match the terms or expressions with their meanings and then use each expression in a sentence.

a)	business speak	e)	go the extra mile
b)	caps	f)	information overload
c)	emoticon	g)	netiquette
d)	EOM	h)	tickle someone's funny bone

1. ___ do more than is expected _____

_____

2. ___ make someone laugh _____

_____

3. ___ graphical representation of emotion _____

_____

4. ___ Internet etiquette _____

_____

5. ___ end of message _____

_____

6. ___ capital letters _____

_____

7. ___ too much information _____

_____

8. ___ communication style using a lot of jargon _____

_____

HRL and Associates

2015, August, 19

Beverley Smith
ABC Hotel
Event Planner
Toronto Ontario
M3A 7K2
1274 Prospect Street

Dear Smith

Subject: change to September sales meeting

We reserved 3 conference rooms for our sale's meeting on sept. 21 we will require an extra room? Would it be possible to have all four room's in the same area of the hotel.

We also require an lcd projector and screen to each room and would like to order Coffee and Pastries for our mid-morning brake

Please say that the extra room is available, and that we can rent the equipment from you. Also please let us know the cost's for the Coffee and Pastires'.

Sincerely

Patricia Oliver
HRL and Associates
Sales Assistant

Language patterns

Complete the definitions and then use each *write* term in a sentence.

1. write down: *record something so you don't forget it*
   There is a memo, so you don't need to write this down.

2. write off: _____

   _____

3. write back: _____

   _____

4. write away: _____

   _____

5. write in: _____

   _____

6. write out: _____

   _____

Vocabulary

Discuss the following vocabulary with your classmates and then use the words to complete the dialogue. One word will be used twice.

business speak	information overload	to whom it may concern
concise	memo	uncluttered
cordial	natural language	until such time
in accordance with	subject line	wordy

Dialogue

Andy	Vincent

Andy: I just can't seem to be able to write a ₁ _____
to my boss this morning.

Vincent: Why is that? Are you suffering from ₂ _____?

Andy: No, it's not that. It's just that I feel nervous whenever I have to send him
anything. He wants me to be more ₃ _____ .

Vincent: How do you start the memo? I hope you don't say ₄ _____ .
That doesn't sound too ₅ _____ .

Andy: No, I don't. But he tells me to make my ₆ _____ more
to the point. I guess I'm too ₇ _____ .

Vincent: That doesn't sound so hard to fix. He's not asking you to go the extra mile. He just wants you to keep it $_8$ _____ .

Andy: Yeah. I know. But he also wants me to avoid using $_9$ _____ and instead use more $_{10}$ _____ .

Vincent: He knows better than you how he wants something sent out.

Andy: But sometimes the sound of $_{11}$ _____ , for example, seems so much more professional than as.

Vincent: $_{12}$ _____ as you become manager, I suggest you write as he has requested.

Writing

CLB 5

From the perspective of a manager, write a memo to your employees outlining a new dress code policy that will take effect immediately.

CLB 6

Write a formal email to a co-worker outlining the details of an upcoming meeting. Address the reader by title; use formal, respectful language; and close with your name and title.

CLB 7

Write a conversational email to a co-worker outlining the details of an upcoming meeting. Include a greeting, write in a friendly but professional tone, and end with a brief and friendly salutation and your first name only.

CLB 8

Write a friendly email to a co-worker outlining the details of an upcoming meeting. Greet the reader casually, use appropriate humour with some jargon and slang, and close with a casual salutation and your first name only.

Group work

Exercise A

In pairs, compose a business letter of two to three paragraphs requesting some changes to an upcoming meeting. Develop a letterhead for your letter. Use block-style format and be sure to check for spelling and grammatical errors.

Exercise B

Match each informal sentence with the corresponding formal sentence.

Informal	Formal
1. _____ Let's consider the options.	a) One might wonder …
2. _____ I want to go out.	b) There is a serious risk of not meeting the deadline.
3. _____ You might wonder …	c) Canadian people tend to do things in their own way.
4. _____ Suki typed the memo.	d) I talked to Joe and his suggestion was to reschedule the meeting.
5. _____ We might not make the deadline.	e) I regret to inform you that I will not be able to attend.
6. _____ We Canadians do things our own way.	f) From which country does she come?
7. _____ I talked to Joe and he suggested we reschedule the meeting.	g) It is important to consider the options.
8. _____ Which country does she come from?	h) The woman whom you are describing is my sister.
9. _____ The woman you are describing is my sister.	i) The memo was typed by Suki.
10. _____ I'm sorry I can't come.	j) I would like to go out.

What strategies were used to make the informal sentences sound more formal?

_____

_____

What other strategies are used to create formality in spoken English?

_____

_____

Formality Hints

- Certain phrases are often used to formalize a sentence. Some examples are, *It is important to ...* and *I regret to inform you ...*

- The passive voice can formalize a sentence. For example, *Yuliya chose Ahmad to be the new assistant* becomes *Ahmad was chosen by Yuliya to be the new assistant.*

- Starting a sentence with *it* or *there* will formalize a sentence. For example, *There is a tendency to underestimate the length of time needed to complete the task.*

- A sentence can be formalized by replacing personal pronouns with *one,* which is a formal version of *you.* For example, *One is hesitant to discuss this with the employer.*

- Formalized vocabulary and complex sentences will formalize a sentence. For example, *This memo is to inform you of the upcoming meeting scheduled for this Thursday in the meeting room.*

- The placement of prepositions and pronouns can make the difference between a formal or an informal sentence. For example, *What are you thinking about?* becomes *About what are you thinking?* and *The woman you spoke to is my boss* becomes *The woman to whom you spoke is my boss.*

On your own

In your notebook, start a list of words and phrases that are considered "business speak." Include the natural vocabulary that would be more appropriate to use instead.

Personal learning: practising English outside of the classroom

This past week I ... _____

Tomorrow I will try ... _____

My favourite new word is ... _____

By next class I will ... _____

Chapter 9

Getting Along with Co-workers

Key Point Focus

- Getting along with others
- Developing and maintaining positive relationships with your co-workers

First things first

Getting along with your colleagues is a big part of any job. Not many people are totally isolated from their co-workers. Here are a few guidelines to remember to help create positive workplace relationships:

Respect your colleagues. Respect their time and space by being thoughtful and courteous. They will appreciate the courtesy.

Be reliable. *Make no promises that you can't keep* is an old saying, but it is still relevant to today's workplace. If you promise to call someone by a certain time, you are expected to accomplish this. Keep your promises and honour your commitments, and you will be seen as a reliable colleague.

Be on time. Punctuality is important. Being on time for a meeting usually means arriving a few minutes before it is scheduled to start so that you have a chance to greet others, find a seat, and organize your things.

Take responsibility. Consider the impact of your own actions. Be helpful and co-operative—if you make a mistake, accept responsibility for your error. Fix it if you can. Resolve not to make that mistake again.

Be a good communicator. Present information clearly and accurately to help others understand. Listen when your colleagues are sharing information with you. Ask questions if you do not understand. Reflect on what you have heard.

Show appreciation. A *thank you* goes a long way toward building mutual respect. Saying *please* and *thank you* helps to build a respectful work environment. This is an important part of developing and maintaining positive workplace relationships.

Exercise A

Underline any vocabulary in First things first that you do not know. Make a list of the words or expressions. In pairs, compare lists. Help each other fill in the definitions for the unfamiliar vocabulary.

Exercise B

Work with your partner to create three additional guidelines to add to the list in First things first.

Exercise C

In pairs, discuss the following situations. Think about similar experiences you may have had in the workplace. What is it about each situation that upsets people?

1. Vince spilled coffee on the kitchen counter and did not clean it up.
2. Karla left the photocopier jammed and out of paper.
3. Alex regularly talks about other people's personal business.
4. Marta is always negative and critical.
5. Frank talks in a very loud voice.
6. Isabel is always late for meetings.
7. Cindy always interrupts and does not let other people talk.

Buzzwords

Exercise A

Match each term or expression with its meaning and then use it in a sentence.

a) in a bind	d) play the devil's advocate
b) in the same boat	e) put people down
c) pain in the neck	f) wake-up call

1. ___ criticize others _____
   _____

2. ___ in a difficult situation that you don't know how to get out of _____
   _____

3. ___ argue against something even though you agree with it _____
   _____

4. ___ person or thing that you find annoying _____
   _____

5. ___ in the same situation _____
   _____

6. ___ experience that causes you to reflect on a situation _____
   _____

Exercise B

Fill in each blank with a buzzword from this chapter.

1. I'm _____ without a car. I drive everywhere.
2. I'm _____ . My car is not working.
3. When my car slid in the snow it was a real _____ .
   It is time to get snow tires.
4. Your new boyfriend is a real _____ . He never fills
   your car with gas after he has used it.
5. Don't _____ . He is trying hard to be considerate.
6. You really don't think that. You just like to _____ .

Exercise C

Negative Descriptions

The following chart contains terms used to describe some types of co-workers that people often try to avoid in workplaces. These descriptions are definitely not compliments. Work with a partner to write definitions and sentences for the following terms.

Negative Term	Meaning	Use in a Sentence
nosy	a person who is too interested in other people's private lives	That salesperson was very nosy—he asked about my personal relationships.
bossy		
whiner		
nitpicker		
chatterbox		
Other negative descriptors you have heard • •		

Exercise D

Make a list of qualities that individuals should possess in order to establish positive work relationships. In pairs, compare your lists. Explain the reasons for your selections.

Language patterns

Make no promises you can't keep is an old motto or saying. A motto is a short sentence or a phrase that expresses a rule of behaviour.

Create your own mottos for positive workplace interactions using the following *make* terms. Compare your results with a partner. Are there any similarities?

Make Term	Your Motto
make a promise	*Make no promises you can't keep*
make an appointment	
make an attempt	
make a mistake	
make an impact	
make an effort	

Look up the word *make* in a phrasal verbs dictionary. What other expressions can be formed with *make*?

Vocabulary

accurate	courtesy	mutual
appreciate	efficient	productive
avoid	error	relevant
colleagues	flexible	reliable
commitment	isolated	vital
confident		

Underline any vocabulary words that you do not know. Make a list of the words. In pairs, compare lists. Help each other fill in definitions for the unfamiliar vocabulary.

Using six of the vocabulary words, write a paragraph to describe a positive work environment.

Dialogue

Fred   Tina

Fred: I'm in a bind without my car. I drive everywhere.

Tina: I'm in the same boat. My car is not working. It's a real pain in the neck being without my car.

Fred: I was not prepared for the weather. I hit an icy patch and my car slid. It was a real wake-up call. I need my snow tires.

Tina: That's scary. Are you okay?

Fred: Yes, I'm just fine. My car isn't. So now I need a ride to Sonia's birthday party. Do you have a ride?

Tina: Yes. Maria has offered me a ride.

Fred: Do you think she'll have enough room for me too?

Tina: I can't make a promise for her. You should call her and ask.

Fred: That's a good idea. That's what I'll do.

Practise the dialogue with a partner.

After you have read through once, underline all the statements in the dialogue. The tone of your voice should fall at the end of each statement. Circle all the questions in the dialogue. The tone of your voice should rise at the end of any question that can be answered with a yes or a no.

Writing
CLB 5

What types of people do you prefer to work with? Write a 150-word paragraph. Remember to include an introduction and a conclusion.

CLB 6

What types of people do you prefer to work with? Write a 250-word paragraph. Remember to include an introduction and a conclusion.

CLB 7

What types of people do you prefer to work with? Write a 300-word paragraph. Describe and compare two different personality types. Remember to include an introduction and a conclusion.

CLB 8

What types of people do you prefer to work with? Write a 400-word paragraph. Describe and compare two different personality types. Remember to include an introduction and a conclusion.

Group work

What types of people do you prefer to work with? In small groups, come up with a list of positive workplace attributes.

Compare your list with another group's. Discuss any new words you do not already have—should they be added to your list?

On your own

What have you learned about the Canadian workplace from this chapter? Reflect on your learning and fill in the table below.

What I Know	What I Want to Know	What I Have Learned

Personal learning: practising English outside of the classroom

This past week I … _____

Tomorrow I will try … _____

My favourite new word is … _____

By next class I will … _____

Chapter 10

Good Boss/Bad Boss

Key Point Focus

- Differentiating between types of managers and working with any of them
- Managing problems with your boss
- Asking for a raise
- Understanding and preparing for a performance review

First things first

Can you recognize what type of boss you have? Good bosses tend to inspire confidence in their employees. Good bosses know what they are talking about. Good bosses have integrity. Good bosses don't micromanage their employees—they let employees work independently. Good bosses are there when you need them.

Bad bosses never seem to be around when they are needed. Bad bosses always want to know what you are doing and want you to justify it. Bad bosses don't smile much and appear to be distrustful. Bad bosses focus on employees' weaknesses rather than strengths.

Exercise A

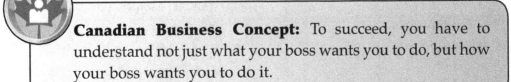

Canadian Business Concept: To succeed, you have to understand not just what your boss wants you to do, but how your boss wants you to do it.

Consider Victoria, the assistant manager at a private art gallery. (*You're Hired...Now What?* p. 215) She enjoyed working with the artists and customers and understood the up-and-down cycles in art sales. Her boss, however, viewed the art gallery as just a business. He was only concerned with how the gallery could sell more art. Discuss what you would do in this situation if you were Victoria.

Exercise B

In pairs, match the characteristics to the different types of bosses.

1. ___ big ego manager
2. ___ competitive manager
3. ___ quick-change artist
4. ___ inexperienced manager
5. ___ micromanager
6. ___ incompetent manager
7. ___ unavailable manager
8. ___ impatient manager
9. ___ screaming or moody manager
10. ___ slave-driver or workaholic boss
11. ___ master/servant boss

a) he asks you to run personal errands

b) he yells at you under stress

c) she expects you to work long hours

d) he lacks skills in technology or operations

e) she wants the spotlight for herself

f) she will think her ideas are better than yours

g) he wants to check every detail of what you do

h) she is a poor communicator and often unavailable

i) he is intense, demanding, and often aggressive

j) he has less talent and knowledge than you

k) she changes her mind and forgets what she told you

Buzzwords

Match the expressions with their meanings and then use each in a sentence. Not all expressions will be used.

a) ace the presentation
b) ASAP
c) baby boomers
d) connect the dots
e) cover for someone
f) go to bat for you
g) heads-up

h) high-maintenance employee
i) hound you
j) pick up the slack
k) stroke someone's ego
l) up in arms
m) want to vent

1. — support you _____
    _____

2. — flatter someone _____
    _____

3. — give a very successful presentation _____
    _____

4. — bother you repeatedly _____
    _____

5. — individuals born between 1946 and 1964 _____
    _____

6. — fill in a shift for an absent employee _____
    _____

7. — as soon as possible _____
    _____

8. — figure out the relationship between two or more things _____
    _____

Language patterns

Complete the definitions and then use each *head* term in a sentence.

1. heads-up: *advance notice of something* _____
    Gordon couldn't remember whether his boss had given him a heads-up about his work
    performance. _____

2. head up something: _____
    _____

3. head honcho: _____
    _____

4. head and shoulders above somebody: _____
    _____

5. head start: _____
    _____

6. head above water: _____
    _____

Vocabulary

assessment	initiative	raise
constructive	probationary period	sandwiched
criticism	promotion	scrapped

Use the words above to complete the following definitions.

1. A process in which a judgment is made about a person or a situation is called an _____ .

2. To show _____ is to start something significant.

3. The time during which an employer can evaluate the work of a new employee is called a _____ .

4. A project is _____ when an employer decides that it is not practical.

5. When a discussion about something is squeezed in between two other major dialogues, we say it is _____ .

6. An upward movement within the company to a more important position is called a _____ .

7. A useful response intended to produce good results is called constructive _____ .

8. An increase in salary based on merit or years of service is called a _____ .

Dialogue

Fill in the blanks using words from the Buzzwords and Vocabulary sections.

Gordon	Dennis

Gordon: I don't understand it. How could I have been fired? My 1 _____ wasn't up yet. My performance review was great. It wasn't like I was a 2 _____ . I wasn't even thinking about asking for a 3 _____ either.

Dennis: Did your boss give you a 4 _____ on areas he wanted to see improved? 5 _____ is a good thing. It can help you improve your work habits.

Gordon: I'm not sure. I can only remember the positive things he said. He must have ₆ _____ the negative remarks in between the positive comments. I was sure I was going to get a

₇ _____ .

Dennis: Would you like me to ₈ _____ ?

Gordon: No, man. I don't want to get you into trouble. You have enough to worry about now that he ₉ _____ your project.

Dennis: Yeah, I did get a bit ₁₀ _____ over that.

Gordon: If you don't mind, I just ₁₁ _____ here. I guess I didn't ₁₂ _____ and ₁₃ _____ where I should have. I didn't show enough ₁₄ _____ . I guess it's too late now to learn from this ₁₅ _____ .

Writing

CLB 5

Write a paragraph describing which type of boss you have. Why do you think this? What are your boss's characteristics?

CLB 6

One day your boss is friendly and easygoing. The next day he's cold as ice. When he's under stress, frustrated, or angry, he yells.

Write a two-paragraph essay explaining how you would handle this situation.

CLB 7

In a three- or four-paragraph essay, outline the steps you would take to ask your boss for a raise.

Use the following tips to help you prepare:
- Find out what to ask for.
- Evaluate your employer's financial health and your industry.
- Prepare your case.
- Set up an appointment with your boss.
- Present your case.
- Think ahead.

Canadian Business Concept: Never ignore areas of improvement that your boss brings up in a performance review.

Review the Dialogue section. How could Gordon have improved his situation? What should he have done? Find out about performance reviews at your place of work. How should you prepare for them? What aspects of your performance will your boss consider when she writes your performance review? Write a summary in which you address the answers to these questions.

Group work
Exercise A

Work in pairs. Discuss the steps you could take to build a positive working relationship with your boss.

Exercise B

Which factors foster a positive working environment in the workplace and motivate employees to do a good job? Is money the main factor?

_____

_____

Exercise C

What does job satisfaction mean to you?

_____

_____

Exercise D

What are the most important attributes of a good boss?

_____

_____

Exercise E

In pairs, discuss the meaning of the saying _When the cat's away, the mice will play_. How might this apply to the workplace? Make a list of behaviours and actions that an employer would disapprove of.

_____

_____

Exercise F

Following a meeting or a conversation with your employer, you may want to recap the discussion with someone else, such as a colleague. This will involve reported speech.

Change the following examples of direct speech to reported speech.

1. Mr. Smith said, "The meeting is at 9:00 on Thursday."
    Mr. Smith said that the meeting would be at 9:00 on Thursday.

2. "How is that report coming along?" asked Mr. Webb.
    _____

3. Mr. Dumont asked, "Will you be finished your analysis by tomorrow's meeting?"
    _____

4. "I'm getting tired of commuting every week," complained Rachel.
    _____

5. "I want to ask Mr. Hanson for a raise," said Shelley.
    _____

6. "Her work on that project is exemplary," said Mr. Huston.
    _____

On your own

Choose one of the two options below and consider the associated questions.

Watch the movie *Working Girl*. What type of boss is Katharine Parker? What characteristics does she exhibit? Would you want to work for her? Why or why not?

or

Watch the movie *The Devil Wears Prada*. What type of boss is Miranda Priestly? What characteristics does she exhibit? Would you want to work for her? Why or why not?

Personal learning: practising English outside of the classroom

This past week I … _____

Tomorrow I will try … _____

My favourite new word is … _____

By next class I will … _____

Chapter 11

Client Relations and Business Etiquette

Key Point Focus

- Making a good impression at a client's office
- Business etiquette in Canada

First things first

In the first 12 seconds of meeting someone, you make a first impression that could significantly impact your business relationship. Just as you form an opinion of your client, your client forms an opinion about you. Your appearance, body language, mannerisms, and level of confidence all influence how your client will think of you.

There are a number of things that you can do to ensure a good first impression. For one thing, be on time. No one appreciates being kept waiting—making someone wait for you is considered rude in Canada. However, that doesn't mean you should be extremely early either. Consider Mitch, who had a 10:00 meeting with a client. (*You're Hired...Now What?* p. 239) He arrived at 9:35. His client was irritated because she felt pressured to see Mitch right away. She may have had other responsibilities that she wanted to complete first. Plan to arrive five to ten minutes prior to your meeting time.

Another thing you can do is to be respectful of office protocol when you have an appointment. Don't assume that the nearest chair and desk are for your use. Your client may have a specific place where he would like you to sit and open your briefcase. Benoit, for example, annoyed his client considerably when he sat down in the nearest chair and spread his papers over the client's desk. (*You're Hired...Now What?* p. 239)

Turn off your cellphone. What will your client think when she sees you already speaking to someone when you are supposed to be meeting with her for the first time? Your client deserves 100 percent of your attention. If you give her anything less, you'll create a less-than-favourable first impression.

Exercise A

"Customers pay the bills—they are the lifeblood of your company."

In small groups, discuss what this means.

Exercise B

With a partner, discuss what you would do in the following situations:

a) You and your client both arrive at the door at the same time.

b) Someone holds the door open for you.

c) You see someone struggling with a package and trying to open the door.

d) Your client offers you a cup of coffee, but you don't drink coffee.

e) You meet someone for the first time.

f) You are invited by a client to a restaurant, but you don't eat that kind of food.

g) You would like a roll with your dinner, but the bread basket is on the other side of the table.

h) Your client asks you a question and you still have a small bit of food in your mouth.

Exercise C

In small groups, decide whether each sentence is true (T) or false (F). Discuss your answers as a class.

1. It is okay to heap your plate with food in a buffet line.	T / F
2. You can return your potato chip to the dip bowl after you have taken a bite.	T / F
3. You shouldn't eat bread or anything else at the table until everyone has arrived.	T / F
4. You should check with the server about how a dish is prepared.	T / F
5. Your client won't mind if you are a few minutes late.	T / F
6. If your guests order alcoholic beverages, you should too.	T / F
7. It is a sign of respect to finish everything on your plate.	T / F
8. It is acceptable to speak with a small bit of food in your mouth.	T / F
9. It is okay to pick at food which is stuck in your teeth.	T / F
10. It is okay to push away your bowl or plate when finished.	T / F
11. It is best to place your client between your partner and yourself at the table.	T / F
12. You should try to encourage your client to choose inexpensive items from the menu.	T / F
13. You should not start to eat your meal until everyone's food has arrived.	T / F

Buzzwords

Match each expression with its meaning and then use it in a sentence. Not all expressions will be used.

a) American and Continental style	g) gender-neutral
b) client-focused	h) left to right
c) customer-centric	i) nibbled on it
d) double-dipping	j) one-on-one
e) going Dutch	k) table manners
f) face-to-face	

1. ___ treating men and women in the same way _____

_____

2. ___ in the same room or place _____

_____

3. ___ placing clients' wishes above all else _____

_____

4. ___ dipping food for a second time, after you've bitten it _____

_____

5. ___ basic styles of business dining _____

_____

6. ___ between two people only _____

_____

7. ___ dining out with the understanding that each individual will pay for his or her own meal _____

_____

8. ___ organized around the needs of customers _____

_____

Language patterns

Complete the definitions and then use each term in a sentence.

1. eat somebody's lunch: *take away another company's business or its share of the market*

Unless we're careful, our international competitors will eat our lunch.

2. eat humble pie: _____

_____

3. eat your words: _____

_____

4. eat your heart out: _____

5. eat somebody alive: _____

_____

6. eat your hat: _____

_____

Vocabulary

Match the vocabulary words with the corresponding pictures. Not all of the words will be used.

appetizer	cultivate	gaffe
blunder	engage	inedible
buffet	faux pas	vegetarian

1. _____

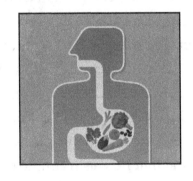

2. _____

3. _____

4. _____

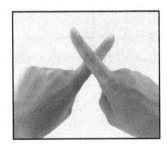

5. _____

6. _____

Dialogue

Fill in the blanks using words from the Buzzwords
and Vocabulary sections.

| Pina | John | Laura |

Pina: Boy! Did I ever ₁ _____ when I went to
dinner last night with my client!

John: What happened?"

Pina: I took him to a chic French restaurant and thought I'd try something
new. I ordered quail hearts. But I couldn't eat them. I found them
₂ _____ .

John: I can share your distress. I made a major ₃ _____
last week when I forgot my ₄ _____ .
Without thinking, I reached across the table for the bread basket
instead of waiting for someone to pass it.

Laura: Well, since we're on the subject, I might as well share my
₅ _____ with you guys. I took my client,
Bob, out for dinner. The menu didn't offer anything for a
₆ _____ , so I didn't order an
₇ _____ . Well Bob did. He felt very
awkward eating alone when I wasn't eating. He was feeling especially
uncomfortable when I kept trying to ₈ _____
him at the same time that he was trying to eat.

Pina: Well, I sure learned that a business dinner is no time to experiment
with new dishes.

John: Here's a little bit of useful advice: Did you know that when you pass
food around, you pass it ₉ _____ ? Who knew?

Laura: Well I learned that I should have ordered something and then just
₁₀ _____ to keep him company. I need to
₁₁ _____ more dining etiquette, or just give
up and eat at a ₁₂ _____ from now on.

Writing

CLB 5

Develop a list of foods that you should avoid eating at a business meeting. In one paragraph, explain why they are problematic.

CLB 6

Canadian Business Concept: When you don't know the restaurants in the area, choose a formal restaurant in one of the better hotels. You will generally have very good service and a large selection of food choices.

Write two paragraphs explaining why this is a good strategy.

CLB 7

In a three-paragraph essay, outline the etiquette you would employ as the host of a business meeting in a restaurant.

CLB 8

Research two or three websites that deal with proper business dining etiquette. Describe and summarize your points in a four-paragraph essay. Remember to include an introduction, develop your main points, and finish with a conclusion.

Group work

Exercise A

In pairs, complete the following crossword.

Across

1. casual conversation
4. not suitable to be eaten
6. embarrassing mistake in protocol
8. stylish
11. pay for your own meal when out with a group: go _____
12. big mistake
13. dipping something into a sauce bowl after you have bitten it
15. rules for eating politely
16. admit that what you said is wrong
17. what someone might say to you if he sees that you are envious of him
18. code of conduct

Down

2. food or drink served before a meal
3. row of people waiting to serve themselves at an informal meal
5. pile; a lot
7. in person
9. eat in small bites
10. organized around the needs of customers
14. between two people only

Exercise B

Develop a list of topics that you would consider appropriate for small-talk at a business meeting. Compare what is considered appropriate in Canada to what is considered appropriate in your native country. Discuss the similarities and differences.

Exercise C

Do some online research to find additional suitable topics for small-talk. Compile a list.

Exercise D

One of the most important skills you will need to develop is the ability to ask open questions—questions that require more than a yes or no answer. You will need to ask open questions in order to engage your clients and draw them into conversations. Look at the following answers. As a group, decide what the corresponding questions could be.

1. I'm a research chemist at the university.
   What do you do? _____

2. I enjoy gardening and reading books. I also like to go on short hikes.
   _____

3. My family's well. They're looking forward to the holidays, though.
   _____

4. I was disappointed with the results. I had really hoped that Canada would win. _____

5. It sure is hot today. I prefer days without humidity.
   _____

6. I became interested in accounting when I was studying at university.
   _____

7. I think the most challenging part of my job is trying to decide when to delegate. _____

8. I've known Tom for over ten years now. We went through university together. _____

9. My hometown is a wonderful place. It's changing now, though, with more and more people moving into the area.
   _____

10. I've never eaten here before. It looks like a wonderful place.
    _____

On your own

Research the restaurants in your area. Ask your peers which restaurants would be appropriate for a formal or informal business meeting.

Personal learning: practising English outside of the classroom

This past week I ... _____

Tomorrow I will try ... _____

My favourite new word is ... _____

By next class I will ... _____

Chapter 12

Office Politics, Gossip, and Romance

Key Point Focus

- Dealing with office politics
- Avoiding office gossip
- Office romance
- Sexual harassment

First things first

Office gossip is inevitable. It exists no matter where you work. But there are strategies you can employ to help you handle the grapevine.

- Take everything you hear with a grain of salt. Before you react to something, make sure that it is true.
- Avoid contributing to the grapevine. Not everyone can be trusted to keep secrets. Can you be sure that your words won't become mangled?
- Make the grapevine work to your advantage. Perhaps you would like to share something positive that you have accomplished. This may trickle up to company executives.
- Avoid using the grapevine to discuss someone who irks you. Doing so is underhanded and not at all professional.
- Be selective about what you discuss—there are topics that run the risk of being taboo in a workplace environment. These include: religion, politics, your sex life, problems with your family, your health problems, and your career aspirations. Save conversations that revolve around these areas for after-hours.
- Walk away or change the subject when someone starts to gossip. By doing so, you distance yourself from the office gossips. Remember, you will be known by the company you keep.

Exercise A

Match each type of office politics with the strategy you could employ to deal with it.

Office Politics	Strategy
1. _____ A co-worker is saying things about you that are not true.	a) Write down your strengths, experience, and job responsibilities. Discuss these in a meeting with your boss. Ask him for the opportunity to use these skills on your next project.
2. _____ A co-worker is attacking your ideas even though he has little talent of his own.	b) In a positive tone of voice, ask the individual to tell you exactly what he doesn't like about your idea. Ask him to help you develop an alternative solution.
3. _____ A co-worker who has done something negative to you tries to shrug off her actions when you confront her.	c) Go directly to your co-worker and ask her why she is saying untrue things about you. Encourage her to talk to you directly if she has any future problems.
4. _____ A co-worker tries to find a way to make you look incapable of doing a job on your own.	d) Minimize interactions with this person. Accept his help if he offers it. Thank him for his contributions in front of your boss.
5. _____ Your employer assigns you to a doomed project that doesn't suit your abilities as a way to get rid of you without actually firing you.	e) Call the individual right away. She will look unprofessional for not providing you with what you need.
6. _____ A co-worker "forgets" to provide you with material you need for a meeting with the boss.	f) Don't argue. Invite the other person to meet with you to try to find a solution to the problem. Document everything.

Exercise B

Categorize the following examples of sexual harassment as Verbal, Non-verbal, Written, Physical, or Visual.

1. Saying, "If I were single, I'd ask you out." _____

2. Saying, "I love your legs in that dress." _____

3. Rubbing up against someone _____

4. Staring at someone's body _____

5. Using a screen saver of a naked man or woman _____

6. Sending an email containing a joke with a sexual connotation _____

7. Touching another employee inappropriately _____

8. Complimenting a co-worker on his or her body _____

9. Impeding or blocking a co-worker's movement _____

10. Repeatedly asking out a co-worker _____

Buzzwords

Match the expressions with their meanings and then use each one in a sentence. Not all expressions will be used.

a)	backstabber	h)	put two and two together
b)	come on to you	i)	snipe
c)	dish the dirt	j)	suck up
d)	ex	k)	the cat will be out of the bag
e)	nitpick	l)	two-faced
f)	object of his affection	m)	underhanded
g)	put out fires		

1. — gossip about someone _____

_____

2. __ insincere or hypocritical _____

_____

3. __ find fault in a petty manner _____

_____

4. __ someone who betrays a friend or co-worker _____

_____

5. __ deceitful _____

_____

6. __ make a sly, critical attack _____

_____

7. __ resolve problems _____

_____

8. __ display exaggerated friendliness _____

_____

Language patterns

Complete the definitions and then use each *cat* term in a sentence.

1. playing cat and mouse with someone: *being sometimes kind, sometimes cruel*
   The company has been playing cat and mouse with its employees since this strike began.

2. cat got your tongue?: _____

_____

3. cat's pajamas: _____

_____

4. let the cat out of the bag: _____

    _____

5. look like something the cat dragged in: _____

    _____

6. like the cat who's stolen the cream: _____

    _____

Vocabulary

Discuss the following vocabulary with your class.

aspiration	irk	trickle
Don Juan	sexual harassment	virtuous
grapevine	taboo	

For each vocabulary word below, several synonyms and one antonym are listed. Circle the antonym, then use the vocabulary word and its antonym in a sentence.

1. irk: irritate, bore, annoy, appease, bother, provoke

    _____

2. trickle: dribble, drip, leak, ooze, flow, seep

    _____

3. taboo: prohibited, restricted, acceptable, banned, forbidden, off limits

    _____

4. virtuous: prudent, trustworthy, inappropriate, moral, honourable, respectable

    _____

5. aspiration: objective, apathy, purpose, intention, scheme, desire

    _____

Dialogue

Fill in the blanks using words from the Buzzwords and Vocabulary sections.

Lydia	Beverley

Lydia: Have you met Adolpho yet? He's all over the ₁ _____ .

Beverley: Have I? Frankly, who hasn't? I think he's asked out every woman in this department. What a ₂ _____ !

Lydia: If you're breathing and female, he'll ₃ _____ in no time.

Beverley: He's so much like my $_4$ _____ that I have a hard time talking to him. That $_5$ _____ me. He'd better be careful.

Lydia: Why do you say that?

Beverley: If he gets persistent with anyone, he could end up crossing a fine line
and be charged with $_6$ _____ .

Lydia: I didn't $_7$ _____ . You're right! He had better be careful.

Beverley: He can't continue like this for too much longer before the

$_8$ _____ .

Lydia: You're right. Sooner or later, the $_9$ _____
will be angry enough to report him.

Writing

CLB 5

Write a paragraph about how gossip has affected you negatively.

CLB 6

Canadian Business Concept: The difference between networking and gossip is that networking is positive communication that builds relationships, while gossip is mainly negative communication about people that has the power to hurt them.

In a two-paragraph essay, explain how an employee could differentiate between networking and gossip. Include examples of each.

CLB 7

Canadian Business Concept: Single co-workers often have casual friendships, but they are still professional. People working in the same department may have meals together, or even get together after-hours. Be careful not to interpret a casual gesture such as an invitation to lunch as a romantic overture.

What problems could arise from finding yourself attracted to a co-worker? What if you are attracted to your employer? Write your answer in a three- or four-paragraph essay.

What steps should you take to stop a situation that you consider harassment?

Group work

Exercise A

To avoid being pulled into the dynamics of office politics or office gossip, you should be aware of the implicit rules that are operating in your workplace environment. Sometimes you can figure out these rules by paying particular attention to the modals that people use when they speak. In the following sentences, decide whether the information being conveyed is a suggestion, a piece of advice, a possibility, or a certainty. Choose the correct modal from the following choices: *may*, *should*, *must*, *could*. What extra bit of information is implied in each sentence without being explicitly stated?

1. He _____ be here by now. He's late for the meeting.
2. You _____ want to be careful about what you say to him.
3. John _____ be exhausted after such a long flight.
4. Debbie was really sick yesterday but she _____ show up for work today. She has an important presentation due.
5. You _____ take your client to the new Italian restaurant that has just opened up. It's getting great reviews.

Exercise B

With a partner, write a dialogue between two employees, one of whom is harassing the other. Present your conversation to the class in a role play.

On your own

Explore the website for your province's human rights commission. What behaviours are deemed to be sexual harassment? Read the policy documents and the explanation of what you need to do if you are harassed.

Personal learning: practising English outside of the classroom

This past week I … _____

Tomorrow I will try … _____

My favourite new word is … _____

By next class I will … _____

Chapter 13

Avoiding and Solving Problems

Key Point Focus

- Appropriate workplace behaviour
- Problem-solving skills
- Dealing with harassment

First things first

Conflict can arise due to any difference between individuals' values, ideas, expectations, opinions, actions, understanding, needs, or wants. Conflicts and misunderstandings can happen in any setting. Difficult people and difficult situations do exist. If conflict is not resolved appropriately, it may negatively affect the workplace.

Generally, people are considered "difficult" if they are rude, abusive, obnoxious, overly critical, aggressive, sarcastic, uncooperative, or whiny. These people are considered "high maintenance" and may sometimes be avoided by their co-workers. When people or situations begin to get difficult to deal with, our own emotions can sometimes get in the way of good problem solving. Aristotle refers to the appropriate expression of feeling in this quote: "Anyone can become angry—that is easy. But to become angry with the right person, to the right degree, at the right time, for the right purpose, and in the right way—that is not within everybody's power and is not easy."

Difficulty in the workplace can occur at organizational, operational, cultural, or interpersonal levels. Harassment may be one of the difficulties that people encounter in the workplace. The human resources departments in large organizations usually have some form of policy for conflict resolution, harassment, and problem solving.

In Canada, employers are required by the *Canada Labour Code* to develop their own harassment policy. Both the *Canadian Human Rights Act* and the *Canada Labour Code* protect employees from harassment related to work. Engaging in problem solving and conflict resolution are two appropriate ways people might choose to respond to difficult workplace situations.

Exercise A

Modal verbs express possibility, permission, and necessity. Underline all of the modal verbs you can find in the First things first section. Compare your list with a partner's. Which modals would you use for polite requests? Which ones would you use to indicate advisability or strong necessity? Read First things first again. Are there any modals that you think could be changed? How would the changes alter the message of the reading?

Exercise B

Work with a partner. Use a dictionary to look up the definitions of *conflict, difficult,* and *harassment*. What are the synonyms for these words? Use each word in a sentence to describe something you have seen or experienced in the workplace.

conflict: _____

_____

difficult: _____

_____

harassment: _____

_____

Exercise C

There are many useful problem-solving techniques that help to resolve workplace issues. Based on your own work experience, what have you learned about problem solving? In small groups, create a chart to record your observations and experiences.

Problem-solving Techniques

Helpful	Not Helpful

Buzzwords

Match each expression to its meaning and then use it in a sentence.

a)	blow off some steam	e)	stir things up
b)	got off on the wrong foot	f)	vent
c)	high maintenance	g)	whine
d)	hot button		

1. __ area of sensitivity_____

   _____

2. __ complain in an annoying voice _____

   _____

3. __ cause trouble _____

   _____

4. __ release energy or emotions by shouting or doing something active

   _____

5. __ release anger verbally _____

   _____

6. __ requiring a lot of help or attention _____

   _____

7. __ started off badly _____

   _____

Language patterns

Complete the definitions and then use each *blow* term in a sentence.

1. blow a fuse: *get very angry*

   It was only a suggestion. There's no reason to blow a fuse.
2. blow hot and cold: _____

   _____

3. blow your chances: _____

   _____

4. blow your own horn: _____

   _____

5. blow your top: _____

   _____

6. blow the whistle: _____

   _____

Vocabulary

Discuss the following vocabulary words with your class.

appropriate: suitable, acceptable, or correct for the particular circumstances

aggressive: angry and behaving in a threatening way; acting with force and determination to succeed

belittle: make somebody (or the things that somebody does) seem unimportant

complaint: a reason for not being satisfied

cooperative: working together with others toward a shared aim, and being helpful by doing what you are asked to do

criticism: an expression of disapproval

criticize: say what you do not like or what you think is wrong about something

deteriorate: become worse

prohibit: prevent something from being done

obnoxious: extremely unpleasant in a way that offends people

rude: showing a lack of respect for other people

sensitive: aware of, and able to understand, other people and their feelings

sarcasm: words that are the opposite of what you mean, used in order to be unpleasant

sarcastic: expressing sarcasm

Exercise A

Work with a partner and decide whether each word is a noun, verb, adjective, or adverb.

Exercise B

Write a paragraph and use six of the vocabulary words to describe a difficult work experience that someone might have. Read your paragraph to a partner.

Exercise C

Use the vocabulary words to complete the following sentences.

1. The plan has met with widespread _____ from the public.
2. The company has been _____ for not doing anything about the problem.
3. The department has received many_____ from customers about the poor service.
4. The high cost of the sports equipment will_____ many people from buying it for their children.
5. He felt that his co-workers constantly_____ his achievements.

6. People sometimes become _____ when they drink a lot of alcohol.

7. Blue jeans are not _____ dress for a formal party.

8. There is no need to be _____. Please tell me what you really think and feel.

9. It is _____ to speak when your mouth is full of food.

Create your own sentences for the five vocabulary words that were not used in the sentences above.

1. _____

2. _____

3. _____

4. _____

5. _____

Dialogue

Juan   Yan

Juan: Yan, how is your project coming along?
Yan: Okay, I guess.
Juan: To be perfectly honest with you, you don't sound okay.
Yan: Oh. I hope I don't sound like <u>a whiner.</u>
Juan: Ah …
Yan: Well, actually, I guess I am having a few problems understanding what I am supposed to do. I seem to have <u>gotten off on the wrong foot</u> with my co-workers. I think the team thinks that I am <u>high maintenance</u>.
Juan: Is there anything I can do to help?
Yan: I don't want <u>to stir things up,</u> but it might help if I could <u>vent</u> to you in confidence and just sort out my thoughts.
Juan: Yes, it might help <u>to blow off some steam</u> in private.
Yan: I would really appreciate your ideas about problem solving.
Juan: How about a short walk today at lunchtime?
Yan: That sounds great. I'll meet you at the side door at noon.

Exercise A

Some buzzwords have been underlined in the dialogue. Replace them with standard words that would convey the same meaning. Rewrite the sentences in your notebook.

For example: a whiner: *I hope I don't sound like <u>someone who is always complaining.</u>*

Exercise B

In pairs, write a continuation of the dialogue. Include details about Yan's problem and Juan's advice. You may want to use the following expressions to start your sentences.

If I were you, I would …	I see what you mean about …
As far as I know, it would be helpful to …	I was wondering if …
As I understand it, you might want to …	You might consider …
Why don't you …?	By the way, have you tried …?
Have you considered …?	

For example: _Have you considered_ asking the team members for their points of view on the project?

Role play the dialogue for your class.

Writing

CLB 5

You are an employer. You have an employee who repeatedly interrupts people during meetings and belittles their comments. In a paragraph, describe what you would do to solve this problem.

CLB 6

Paul is a co-worker who always interrupts you and belittles your comments. In two paragraphs, describe what you will do to deal with him. How will you solve this problem?

CLB 7

In a three-paragraph essay, define _constructive criticism_ and describe how it can play a positive role in helping employees to improve. How is constructive criticism different from criticism? What are the behavioural outcomes of both of these?

CLB 8

In a three- or four-paragraph essay, describe the steps you would take to handle an angry outburst from a co-worker and an angry outburst from your employer.

Group work

Exercise A

Here are some tips for problem solving in the workplace. Which five do you think are most important? In the first column, put an asterisk (*) next to each of these. Which suggested action do you think should occur first? Rank your top five suggestions in chronological order. In the last column, write *#1* for the first thing that should be done, *#2* for the second, and so on.

Top Five Tips	Problem-Solving Tips	Conversation Suggestions	Rank in Order
	Speak calmly and clearly to explain the problem	• I think we need to clarify ... • I'd like to talk about ...	
	Define the problem.	• What are the symptoms of the problem? • What is the real cause of the problem? • What are the challenges?	
	Create an action plan.	• These are the things we need to do in order to achieve our objectives.	
	Don't assume others see things from your point of view.	• I'd like to hear your perspective on this problem. • What do you think? • How do you see this problem?	
	Be ready and willing to listen.	• I see what you mean ... • Please tell me more about ...	
	Practise the conversation with a trusted friend.	• I would like to say this. How does it sound to you? Is it clear? Is it appropriate?	
	Discuss the concern with a supervisor or the human resources department.	• I was wondering if you have a moment to talk about ...	
	Select a solution.	• Which solution will be best overall? • Are there more approaches that we should consider? • Which one will have the greatest impact? • Which one will be most helpful for the future? • Which one is most helpful right now?	
	Ask the other person for his or her point of view.	• How do you see the problem? • What are the potential solutions? • Are there other things you think we need to consider?	
	Acknowledge the help of others.	• Thank you so much for your ideas.	
	Try to understand the problem.	• Do I have all the information I need?	
	Add your own tip:		

In small groups, take turns explaining the reasons for your selections and the rankings. After your discussion, decide whether you would like to make any changes to your chart.

Are there any other problem-solving tips you think should be added to the list? Add them to the last row of the chart.

Exercise B

In small groups, answer these questions. Use the Vocabulary words and Buzzwords from this chapter.

1. What types of people are the most difficult to work with?
2. Make a list of positive words to describe people who are helpful and enjoyable to work with. What types of people do you like to work with?

Exercise C

You will occasionally have to deal with problematic situations in the workplace. Often, people will give you advice on how to handle these situations, using conditional sentences.

For example: *If I were you, I'd think about contacting human resources for assistance.*

Complete the following conditional sentences.

1. You can have the first break if you _____ (like).
2. If you _____ (ask) me, I'd do it right away.
3. Do you mind if I _____ (leave) early today?
4. If he's late again, _____ .
5. Would you mind if I _____ ?
6. What would have happened if _____ ?
7. If it weren't for the fact that _____ .
8. He'll be very upset if _____ .
9. I was wondering if _____ .
10. If she were here, _____

Look at each sentence you have written again. How would the tone change if the if clause were placed at the beginning of the sentence?

Note: In spoken form, *If you like* is another way of saying *If you want to*. *If you ask me* is another way of saying *I think*.

Exercise D

argumentative	cooperative	positive
rude	hardworking	reliable
confident		

Complete the sentences using the words above.

1. If you keep your promises, you are ——————————— .
2. If you put a lot of effort into your work, you are ——————— .
3. If you interrupt others when they are talking, you are ——————— .
4. If you are willing to work with other people, you are ——————— .
5. If you always disagree with the things other people say, you are

 ——————— .

On your own

1. Search for the CHRC website. What does the acronym CHRC stand for? What information about workplace difficulties can you find on this website?
2. Ask your supervisor or human resources department about professional development opportunities. Does your company offer courses in problem solving, conflict resolution, or difficult communications?

Personal learning: practising English outside of the classroom

This past week I should have … ———————————————

Tomorrow I might try … ——————————————

A positive approach to problem solving would be to … ———————

By next class, I will … ———————————————

Chapter 14

Networking, Small-talk, and Relationship Building

Key Point Focus

- Networking as a communication skill
- Building professional relationships
- Appropriate topics for small-talk
- Networking by connecting with colleagues.

First things first

What does *networking* really mean? Is it more than smiling, shaking hands, and handing out and collecting as many business cards as possible? Yes it is.

Networking is a face-to-face communication skill that will help you develop and maintain business relationships. It involves both give and take. On the one hand, it involves giving attention to another person and on the other hand, it involves taking away information and the potential of a new business relationship.

Connecting with other people is a big part of building work relationships and friendships. Making sure that each connection is a positive and effective one is both an art and skill. Networking involves being friendly, being willing to listen, and knowing how to use small-talk effectively.

Generally, small-talk does not involve potentially controversial topics, such as anyone's weight or age, religion, politics, sex or gender issues, personal family problems, and health problems. Starting conversations with people you do not know can be challenging, but you can prepare yourself. Prior to a networking event, read the newspaper for local, national, and international news. Read some current business magazine articles, and try to become familiar with recent sporting events, movies, and television programs. Be ready to listen to others and share your perspective.

In Canada, networking occurs not only at professional associations and meetings, but also at parties and social gatherings. In both social and business situations, networking can be used to connect with colleagues and to build professional relationships.

Canadian Business Concept: Once you join a networking group, you'll hear about other similar organizations. Most people who network belong to more than one group, and most groups are interested in increasing their membership.

Exercise A

What topics would you consider inappropriate for small-talk? Do you think that different cultures have different understandings about what is appropriate and inappropriate for topics of conversation? Discuss your opinion with the class.

Exercise B

In pairs, write two questions and two statements that would be appropriate for beginning a conversation at a networking event.

Join with another group and take turns starting a conversation with your questions or statements. Which comments or questions were most successful? Why do you think they worked well?

Exercise C

Some "safe" topics for small-talk are the weather, transportation to work, travel, hobbies, restaurants, movies, magazine articles, community news, shopping, car maintenance, and television programs. With a partner, make a list of other safe topics.

Complete each of the following sentences by sharing your opinion on a safe topic.

For example,

- I enjoy _watching nature documentaries on TV._
- I prefer the _snow to the icy rain._
- I find it a challenge to _drive on ice without my snow tires._
- Getting to work today was _a real headache with all the spring road construction._

I enjoy _____.

I prefer _____.

I find it a challenge to _____.

Getting to work today was _____.

It's interesting that you mentioned _____.

Exercise D

With a partner, change the statements from Exercise C into questions to create conversation starters.

For example,

- _Did you see_ the nature documentary last night on TV?

Here are some more sample questions. Fill in the blanks using situations from your own experience.

Did you see the article in the _____?

Did you see the notice on the staff bulletin board about the _____

_____?

How do you like the _____so far?

What did you think about the_____?

Buzzwords

Exercise A

Match each expression with its meaning then use the expression in a sentence.

a)	after-hours	e)	mix and mingle
b)	boost you up the ladder	f)	small-talk
c)	give-and-take	g)	two's company, three's a crowd
d)	in someone else's shoes	h)	work the room

1. __ listening to other people's points of view and changing your demands if necessary _____

   _____

2. __ after a workplace's period of regular scheduled hours _____

   _____

3. __ polite conversation about unimportant things _____

   _____

4. __ meet and talk with different people at social events _____

   _____

5. __ help you achieve career advancement _____

   _____

6. __ two people are happier alone than in a group of three _____

   _____

7. __ in someone else's situation _____

8. __ make conversational connections with many people at an event or social gathering _____

Exercise B

Think about the last time that you had the opportunity to network. What strategies did you use? In a small group, discuss possible networking strategies. Use as many buzzwords and ideas from the the First things first section as possible.

Language patterns

Some expressions help to show the relationship between ideas.

Exercise A

On the one hand is an expression that is used to balance two ideas that contrast and oppose, but do not contradict each other. The order of the ideas or facts does not matter.

Networking, <u>on the one hand</u>, involves giving attention to someone else. <u>On the other hand</u>, it involves taking away information and the potential of a new business relationship.

<u>One the one hand</u>, I love watching the snowflakes fall but <u>on the other hand</u>, I don't like shovelling all that snow.

Use the statements below to create *on the one hand ... on the other hand* sentences.

1. Canada's climate can be unpredictable. Rothsay, New Brunswick, has a cold, snowy winter. Victoria, British Columbia, has a mild, rainy winter.

2. Winnipeg is known for its cold winter winds. Winnipeg has many underground passageways connecting stores and businesses.

3. Halifax has a busy tourist area around the harbour. Halifax has a beautiful quiet park in the middle of the city

4. Toronto has a large population. Toronto offers many leisure activities.

5. Europe covers a lot of territory on a map. Europe has an extensive train system.

_____

_____

_____

_____

Create four additional *on the one hand … on the other hand* sentences using your own ideas. Check your sentences with a partner to make sure that the ideas contrast but do not contradict each other.

_____

_____

_____

_____

Exercise B

Not only … but also is another more formal expression that helps show the relationship between ideas.

In Canada, networking occurs <u>not only</u> at professional associations and meetings, <u>but also</u> at parties and social gatherings.

The team meeting was <u>not only</u> very brief, <u>but also</u> very helpful.

Last week was <u>not only</u> hot, <u>but also</u> humid.

Create four *not only … but also* sentences, using your own ideas. Check your sentences with a partner to make sure that the statements show the relationship between ideas.

_____

_____

_____

_____

Vocabulary

Discuss the following vocabulary with your class.

align	controversial	networking
chat	crucial	prior
connect	mentoring	relationships
connection	mingle	socializing

Read First things first again. Underline any vocabulary that you do not know and make a list of these words or expressions. Compare lists with a partner. Help each other fill in the definitions for the unknown vocabulary.

Write a paragraph using six of the vocabulary words above to describe the most important things to remember about networking.

Dialogue

Use the Vocabulary words to fill in the dialogue. Discuss the meanings of any words that are not used in the dialogue.

Nancy   Jorge

Nancy: Hello. Welcome to our monthly ₁ —————————————————— event. My name is Nancy.

Jorge: Hello. I'm Jorge. This is my first time here.

Nancy: Well Jorge, this is my first time as ₂ —————————————————— . But I have been a member of this organization for three years and have been able to ₃ —————————————— with many people through this ₄ —————————————— .

Jorge: I am hoping to do some ₅ —————————————————— and begin to ₆ —————————————————— some community business relationships.

Nancy: Yes, these networking events do provide an opportunity to ₇ —————————————————— with others in our field.

Jorge: Yes, I can see that.

Nancy: It's been a pleasure talking to you. Help yourself to some coffee. You have a little time to mix and ₈ —————————————————— before we get started.

Jorge: Thanks. It was nice meeting you too.

Writing

CLB 5

Write a 150-word guide on "How to Network Effectively." Give your advice as a sequence of events. What do you need to understand or do first?

CLB 6

Write a 200-word guide on "How to Network Effectively." Give your advice as a sequence of events. What do you need to understand or do first?

CLB 7

Write a 300-word proposal persuading an organization to host a "How to Network Effectively" event. Describe the advantages to the organization.

CLB 8

Write a 400-word proposal persuading an organization to host a networking event. Describe the advantages to the organization. Include relevant details.

Group work

Exercise A

Canadian Business Concept: Whenever possible, eat before you arrive at the event, or sit down and eat and then get up and network. Networking is about meeting people, not about the food.

In what way are the expectations at a networking event in Canada the same as or different from other cultures?

Exercise B

On a piece of paper, write down a statement that you would be comfortable sharing about your hobbies, sports activities, volunteer activities, reading interests, or travel plans.

In small groups, take turns reading your statements and asking small-talk questions.

Here are a few examples to get you started:

- How did you get interested in that?
- How did you find out about that?
- What made you consider doing that?

- What made you think about that?
- How long have you been involved in that?
- How did you get started with that?

Exercise C

Survey your classmates to find out the names of their favourite TV programs. Make a chart to categorize their answers.

Type of Program	Name of Program (Person 1)	Name of Program (Person 2)	Name of Program (Person 3)
Documentary			
Drama			
Reality			
Sitcom			
Talk show			
Mystery			
Cooking			
Quiz			
Other			

In small groups, discuss you findings. How could you use this information to help create connections and social conversations?

On your own

1. Look up *Citizenship and Immigration Canada* online. What information does the website have about newcomer services in your province?
2. Read the local newspaper for sporting and charity events.
3. Watch the local news to find out about community concerns.
4. Look up your local board of trade and chamber of commerce in the phone book. Call them. What information and services do they offer to the community?

Personal learning: practising English outside of the classroom

This past week I ... _____

The local newspaper is called ... _____

New idioms I will try to use this week ... _____

By next class I will use small-talk to ... _____

Chapter 15

Managing Your Time and Being Productive

Key Point Focus

- Time management and personal organization
- Time-management techniques
- Your organizational priorities

First things first

Time is measured in minutes, hours, days, and years. In western cultures, time is a tangible resource. In both business and social situations, promptness is seen as a sign of courtesy and respect. The abilities to be on time, be organized, be efficient, and set priorities are considered valuable assets in the Canadian workplace.

Good time-management skills will help you control how you use your time and resources. Time itself cannot be controlled—there are always only 24 hours in a day. Life and work can become very busy.

Planning is an important time-management technique. Here are a few tips to get you started:

- Clarify and define your goals. What is it that you hope to achieve?
- Make a to-do list. What things do you need to do to achieve your goal?
- Prioritize your list. What needs to be done first? Make it #1.
- Do the things on your list in order of priority. Make a schedule.
- Monitor and evaluate your progress.

Sometimes how you use your time is not under your own control. There may be outside demands and deadlines that you are not able to change. Other times, time management is a question of personal priorities. What is most important? Is everything that is urgent really important? How is someone supposed to select what is the right thing to do?

Managing how you control your time is an ongoing process. Time management and personal organization are valued workplace attributes.

Exercise A

Write a short paragraph about your time-management skills. How would you describe yourself? Refer to the First things first section for vocabulary and ideas. Discuss your paragraph with a partner.

Exercise B

Canadian Business Concept: Whatever else you do on the job in Canada, be on time! You'll earn a reputation of being organized and considerate, which will go a long way toward helping you succeed in your job.

Many workplaces have punch clocks to get an accurate and reliable account of the employees' hours spent at work. Employees may have to punch in and out several times a day. Other workplaces have scheduled work hours and employees are expected to arrive on time. "On time" often means five to ten minutes before the actual start of the scheduled hours.

In pairs, discuss how different cultures approach time. How could this affect your job in Canada? Make a list of the pros and cons of viewing time as a limited valuable resource.

Exercise C

In pairs, discuss the difference between the two statements below. How do these statements fit in with what you know about the Canadian workplace? Which of these statements is more important to the Canadian workplace?

1. Do things right.	2. Do the right things.

Buzzwords

Exercise A

Use the following terms and expressions to complete the sentences below.

keep your eye on the ball	on the back burner	to-do list
missed the boat	pro and cons	workaholic
mission impossible		

1. People who feel they need to work all the time are called _____ .
2. There is no way I can finish this huge report today. It is a _____ .
3. I consider myself very organized and effective today because my _____ is all completed.

4. You will have to consider all the _____ before you make your decision.

5. You need to remember your goals, stay focused, and _____ .

6. That proposal was due last week, I am afraid we have _____ .

7. We have no time right now to discuss that idea. We will have to put it _____ until our next meeting.

Exercise B

Write a sentence to show that you understand the meaning of each word or phrase.

missed the boat

> *I'm afraid I missed the boat on that proposal—I did not understand what the client wanted and was not able to get it in on time.*

workaholic

_____

_____

keep your eye on the ball

_____

_____

on the back burner

_____

_____

mission impossible

_____

_____

Language patterns

Types of time are often expressed using an adjective followed by the word *time*. Below are a few examples.

Free time: not scheduled, available *I have some free time after lunch. We could meet then.*

Spare time: extra, not scheduled *What are you doing in your spare time this weekend?*

Limited time: small amount *This sale is available for a limited time.*

Vacation time: scheduled holiday *I have vacation time coming up in July.*

Leisure time: relaxation and hobbies *My leisure time activities include golf and swimming.*

Other *time* word patterns can be found in the *Oxford Collocations Dictionary for Students of English.*

Write a paragraph about your plans for your next vacation. Include as many *time* word patterns as you can. Read your paragraph to a partner. Working with your partner, create a sentence for each of the words you were not able to use in either of your paragraphs.

Vocabulary

consider	evaluate	reliable
define	monitor	reputation
effective	prioritize	schedule
efficient	process	tangible
establish	procrastinate	

Using eight of the vocabulary words, write a paragraph to describe how to manage one's time in the workplace.

In pairs, share and discuss time management ideas. Do you think that time management is a North American concept? How do other cultures approach the concept of time? Use the vocabulary words in your discussion.

Dialogue

Jim   Rebecca

Jim: Hi Rebecca. Do you have a moment?
Rebecca: Hello Jim. Sure.
Jim: Great! I have a big project to get out by the end of the week. I need some extra help. Do you have some spare time to help me?
Rebecca: I'd be happy to help you, Jim. However, I will need to consult with my boss, Maria. I am still new here. She may have already organized priorities for my schedule in the next few days.
Jim: Oh, that's okay, then. I will try to find out if anyone else has some free time.
Rebecca: Okay.

In pairs, discuss the dialogue.

- Did Jim make a reasonable request?
- Did Rebecca respond in a responsible way?
- What other things could Jim have said?

Write a new dialogue in which Jim agrees to talk to Rebecca's boss about her schedule. Include words from both the Buzzwords and Vocabulary sections. Role play the dialogue for other groups in the class.

Writing

CLB 5

Identify a workplace goal. Write a to-do list with specific tasks that your goal requires. Describe the steps you will need to take to accomplish your goal.

CLB 6

Identify a workplace goal. Write a to-do list with specific tasks that your goal requires. Provide a detailed description of the steps you will need to take to accomplish your goal.

CLB 7

Identify two workplace goals. Write a to-do list with specific tasks that your goals require. Provide a detailed description of the steps you will need to take to accomplish your goals.

CLB 8

Identify three workplace goals. Write a to-do list with specific tasks that your goals require. Provide a detailed description of the steps you will need to take to accomplish your goals.

Group work

Exercise A

Create a pie chart to show your use of time. The whole chart represents 24 hours. Choose one day from the past week and divide the graph so you can chart your day. How many hours did you spend doing each of the following things?

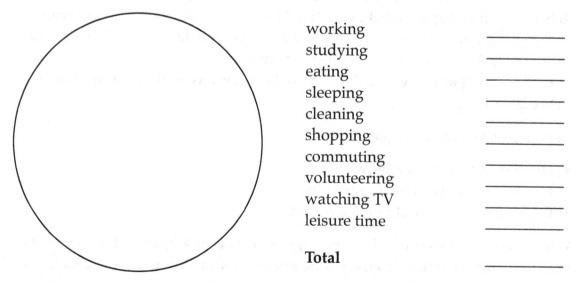

working	_____
studying	_____
eating	_____
sleeping	_____
cleaning	_____
shopping	_____
commuting	_____
volunteering	_____
watching TV	_____
leisure time	_____
Total	_____

(Your list should not add up to more than 24 hours for one day!)

Compare lists with a partner. How are they the same? How are they different?

Exercise B

Many time-management books mention using SMART goals as way to monitor and evaluate your goals. In small groups, discuss your goals and then fill in the following SMART goals chart.

SMART Goals

S: Specific
A goal is something you hope to achieve. What is your goal? Be very specific in stating your goal. _____

_____

M: Measurable
What standard can you use to measure whether or not you have achieved your goal?

_____

A: Attainable
What steps do you need to put in place to work toward this goal?

_____

R: Realistic
The goals must be something that you are able to do. How do you know this goal is realistic?

_____

T: Timely
Create a timeframe for your goal. When do you hope to have it accomplished?

_____

What are the obstacles to your goal?

_____

What do you need to do to deal with the obstacles?

_____

On your own

1. Do an online search for *time management tips*. Make a list of your favourite tips and take it to class with you. Share your information with your classmates.
2. Look in newspapers and professional journals for articles on time management. What time-management suggestions did you find?

Personal learning: practising English outside of the classroom

Something new that I have learned about Canadian workplace culture is …

_____

My favourite new word is … _____

Time management is … _____

By next class I will … _____

Chapter 16

Business Outside the Office

Key Point Focus

- The ins and outs of business travel
- What to expect at trade shows and conferences
- Parties, dinners, and other events

First things first

Canadian Business Concept: Travelling to conferences and trade shows gives you the opportunity to build closer relationships with your company members and to broaden your horizons as you meet other people in your industry.

Travelling for your company can be a very rewarding experience. But there are several things you need to consider in order to make it a successful experience.

- **Be professional** at all times. You are representing your company, and people will judge your company by the way you act.
- **Dress appropriately.** Pay attention to the clothes you wear. Are your clothes pressed and your shoes polished?
- **Keep in touch with your boss.** Maintain updated email or voicemail contact.
- **Watch your expenses.** Small expenses add up and you might not realize how much you add to the bill when you use the room's phone or take food from the fridge. Make sure that you keep all the receipts from any expenses that you incur.

Exercise A

The following chart contains the professions of some people in the travel industry whom you may encounter while on business trips. In pairs, determine what people with these job titles do. Decide how much you would tip each of them.

Job Title	Job Description	Tip
Porter		
Doorman		
Bellhop		
Concierge		
Taxi driver		
Room service attendant		
Valet parking attendant		

Exercise B

Match the travel safety information with the pictures.

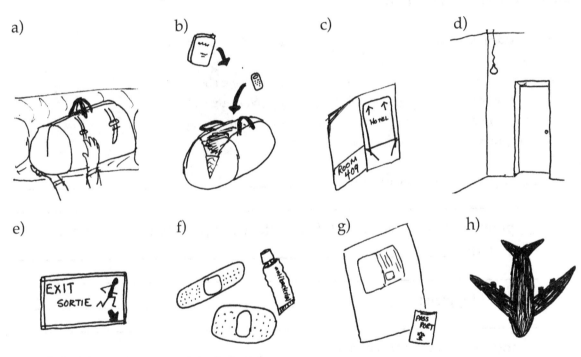

a)   b)   c)   d)

e)   f)   g)   h)

1. Confirm flights, hotel reservations, and business appointments. _____
2. Avoid rooms at the end of long, winding hallways. _____
3. Transfer everything to your carry-on bag before walking through the metal detector. _____
4. Stow your belongings in the overhead bin across the aisle from your seat. _____
5. Know where the closest exits are to your hotel room. _____
6. Photocopy all of your contact information and leave it with a family member. _____
7. Make sure the hotel staff doesn't announce your room number out loud. _____
8. Keep an emergency first aid kit in your briefcase. _____

Exercise C

Juanita was excited about travelling to her first business meeting in another city. (*You're Hired...Now What?* p. 340) The flight arrived on schedule, but Juanita's luggage didn't. She was missing several items she needed, and she felt uncomfortable. This affected the presentation she was making. What could Juanita have done to avoid this scenario?

_____

_____

_____

Buzzwords

Match the expressions with their meanings and then use each in a sentence. Not all expressions will be used.

a)	broaden your horizons	g)	road warriors
b)	BYO	h)	RSVP
c)	carry-on bag	i)	talking shop
d)	eat and run	j)	wake-up call
e)	home away from home	k)	wet blanket
f)	pig out		

1. ___ expand your possibilities: _____

_____

2. ___ phone call from the hotel staff to wake you up at the time you have requested: _____

_____

3. ___ hand luggage: _____

_____

4. ___ individuals who travel a lot: _____

_____

5. ___ place where you feel as comfortable and happy as you do in your own home: _____

_____

6. ___ reply to an invitation: _____

_____

7. ___ leave shortly after eating: _____

_____

8. ___ someone who prevents other people from enjoying themselves:

_____

_____

Language patterns

Complete the definitions and then use each *road* term in a sentence.

1. off the road: *needing to be repaired*

    We'll have to go by bus—my car's off the road at the moment.

2. on the road: _____

    _____

3. on the road to recovery: _____

    _____

4. on the road to ruin: _____

    _____

5. one for the road: _____

    _____

6. road hog: _____

    _____

Vocabulary

Discuss the following vocabulary with your class.

compensate	fiasco	mini-bar
dress code	incur	receipts
expenses	itinerary	tipsy
facilities		

Match the vocabulary words to the pictures below and then use each word in a sentence.

1. _____   2. _____   3. _____   4. _____

5. _____   6. _____   7. _____   8. _____

1. _____
2. _____
3. _____
4. _____
5. _____
6. _____
7. _____
8. _____

Dialogue

Fill in the blanks using words from the Buzzwords and Vocabulary sections.

| Sandra | Bill |

Sandra: Bill, I feel so stupid.

Bill: Why, Sandra?

Sandra: I still can't forget my 1 _____ at the "tropical island" company party.

Bill: Don't worry about it, Sandra. It doesn't matter.

Sandra: Not only did I not check about the 2 _____, but I then tried to compensate by 3 _____ at the 4 _____ . So there I am dressed all wrong and getting 5 _____ . I was on the road to ruin.

Bill: If it makes you feel any better, remember I told you that I was planning a get-together with some of the employees who have come from other cultures?

Sandra: Yes. I assumed that you had had a great time 6 _____ .

Bill: Well, I didn't do my homework. In Canada, we start with the meal and then proceed to the socializing. But in their country, you start with the socializing and conclude with the meal. So everyone

7 _____ .

Sandra: Oh, Bill. I'm so sorry.

Bill: I also didn't explain the dinner clearly. The employees assumed that it was a 8 _____ so they arrived with all kinds of delicious food. It made them feel uncomfortable when I proceeded to bring out all of my food as well. I'm sure I was a

9 _____ after that.

Writing

CLB 5

Develop a flyer advertising a company picnic. Decide what the occasion for the picnic is and illustrate your flyer accordingly. Include all relevant information such as the name of the event, the date and time of the event, the location, and the RSVP information.

CLB 6

You had dinner at your boss's house last night. Write a thank-you letter to show your appreciation for the invitation to your boss's home.

CLB 7

You are attending an office cocktail party. Write a short dialogue between you and a co-worker. Remember that this is an opportunity to make pleasant small-talk and to get to know your peers in a relaxed social situation.

CLB 8

Do some online research to find out what to take on a business trip. In three paragraphs, describe what you would bring and why. Consider all possibilities.

Group work

Exercise A

In small groups, imagine that you are the managers of a local hotel. Discuss which facilities and services you would advertise in order to encourage businesses to hold trade shows or conferences at your hotel.

Exercise B

Business cards serve many purposes, particularly letting others know what you do and how to contact you. With a partner, design your own business cards for a company of your choosing. What information should be on the cards?

Exercise C

You have been invited to a co-worker's home. You may be served food that is new to you. Discuss some tips for eating unfamiliar foods.

Exercise D

You may find yourself in business situations where you need to either confirm information or indicate agreement. Tag questions are a quick and easy way to do these things. Start with a statement, then simply add the negative of the statement's verb to make it into a question. Some sentences require the use of the verb *to do*. Remember to consider the tense of the verb as well. Add tags to the following questions.

1. That was a fabulous dinner, *wasn' it* _____ ?
2. It's two hours by train, _____ ?
3. Our plane will leave at 8:30 p.m., _____ ?
4. We accomplished a lot in the meeting, _____ ?
5. I'm invited too, _____ ?
6. We have a lot to do tomorrow, _____ ?

On your own

Watch the comedy *Planes, Trains and Automobiles*. What calamities happen to the characters during their journey? Would you enjoy this type of business trip? Why or why not? Discuss your reaction with your class.

Personal learning: practising English outside of the classroom

This past week I … _____

Tomorrow I will try … _____

My favourite new word is … _____

By next class I will … _____

Chapter 17

Meetings and Presentations

Key Point Focus

- Planning and organizing meetings
- Making presentations
- Speaking effectively in meetings and presentations

First things first

Conducting an effective meeting requires effort and planning. Here are some tips to help you plan a successful meeting.

- Don't schedule a meeting to discuss information that would be better presented in a memo, email, or brief report. Does the information require a dialogue between people or can it just be disseminated?
- Create an agenda with clear objectives. The more focused your meeting objectives are, the more likely the meeting attendees will be to stay on task and achieve the objectives.
- Ensure that the attendees have read the agenda prior to the meeting. On the agenda, clearly indicate the objectives for the meeting, a list of the topics to be covered, and a list stating who will address each topic and for how long. Provide any additional information that you feel is relevant to the discussion of these agenda items. Adhere to this agenda. Don't allow people to veer off-topic.
- Assign meeting preparation tasks. For example, for problem-solving meetings, ask staff to come to the meeting prepared to offer solutions to the problem. This will get everyone thinking about the meeting topic. By the end of the meeting, make a decision about how you are going to act on the problem. Assign individuals to follow through on particular tasks.
- Allow for an end-of-meeting reflection to discuss what worked well in the meeting. Ask attendees to provide suggestions on how to improve the next one.

Exercise A

Match each type of meeting with its description.

1. departmental meeting _____
2. project meeting _____
3. crisis meeting _____
4. problem or issue meeting _____
5. presentation _____
6. conference call _____
7. conference or seminar _____

a) formal educational event presented by an industry expert
b) meeting called to solve a specific issue
c) meeting that deals with work in progress, and usually happens monthly
d) meeting called to solve a business or company crisis
e) meeting focused on a specific project
f) guest speaker discussing a specific topic
g) teleconference for people in different locations

Exercise B

Canadian Business Concept: In some cultures, employees are not encouraged to debate problems or challenge their managers. In Canada, everyone who attends a meeting is expected to participate and contribute in a positive way. Employees are encouraged to bring up new ideas or suggest alternative ideas—as long as this is done respectfully.

You have called a meeting for 9:00 a.m. At 9:10, people are still straggling in. Some have read the agenda, others haven't. When the meeting begins, one of your colleagues brings up an irrelevant point and it consumes 15 minutes. At the end of the meeting, another meeting has to be scheduled because a key topic wasn't covered. What could you do to ensure that the next meeting is a productive use of everyone's time?

_____

_____

Exercise C

You are attending a departmental meeting. What can you do to ensure that you are a productive participant?

Buzzwords

Match the expressions with their meanings and then use each in a sentence. Not all expressions will be used.

a)	anecdote	h)	lose track
b)	bring something to the table	i)	problem at hand
c)	call to action	j)	ramble off on another topic
d)	doodle	k)	sidetracked
e)	drone on	l)	slow talker
f)	flip chart	m)	wrap up
g)	hijack a meeting		

1. __ short true account or story _____

_____

2. __ speaker who takes too long to make a point _____

_____

3. __ diverge from the main issue _____

_____

4. __ large pad of paper on a stand _____

_____

5. __ scribble or draw absent-mindedly _____

_____

6. __ initiate a solution to a problem _____

_____

7. __ take control and change the direction of a meeting _____

_____

8. __ problem being discussed _____

_____

Language patterns

Complete the definitions and then use each *speak* term in a sentence.

1. speak your mind: *say exactly what you think in a very direct way*
   I like an employee who speaks his mind. _____

2. speak for itself: _____

_____

3. speak for yourself: _____

_____

4. speak too soon: _____

   _____

5. speak volumes: _____

   _____

6. speak highly of somebody: _____

   _____

Vocabulary

Discuss the following vocabulary words with your class.

accent	digress	teleconference
adhere	dissemination	voice distractor
agenda	engage	

Use each vocabulary word in a sentence.

1. accent _____
2. adhere _____
3. agenda _____
4. digress _____
5. dissemination _____
6. engage _____
7. teleconference _____
8. voice distractor _____

Dialogue

Fill in the blanks using words from the Buzzwords and Vocabulary sections.

Hans	Lin

Hans: Oh, man! I'm so nervous.

Lin: Why, Hans?

Hans: I'm giving a presentation at 10:00 a.m. to update the sales and
marketing personnel on my research. I am so worried that I'm going to
_____ of what I'm discussing.

Lin: Why would you think that you would ₂ _____ ?"

Hans: When I'm nervous, I start to speak more quickly, which isn't a good
thing with my ₃ _____ . I forget where I'm at
so I start to say *uh* or *um* to give myself a chance to catch my thoughts
again.

Lin: Let me tell you about my experience giving a presentation when I first started working for the company. Whenever I 4 ——————————————— , I could see people looking at their watches, hoping the meeting would 5 ——————————————— soon. I was so hesitant in my speech that I took forever. In other words, I 6 ——————————————— . I could not 7 ——————————————— the audience at all. Their rolling eyes spoke volumes. I kept thinking it would have been better to set up a 8 ——————————————— instead.

Hans: What did you do about this?

Lin: Voice coaching helped me a lot. It helped me speak with confidence and get rid of those annoying 9 ——————————————— that are troubling you too.

Hans: That sounds like a great idea! I'll look into lessons right away. Thank you so much, Lin.

Lin: You're welcome, Hans.

Writing

CLB 5

You are the manager of a hotel. Prepare an agenda for an upcoming meeting to discuss customer dissatisfaction with the cleanliness of the hotel rooms.

CLB 6

Write a telephone dialogue between a company receptionist and a client. The client would like to arrange a meeting with a company executive to discuss a new project for increasing auto sales.

CLB 7

In paragraph form, outline the steps you would take to plan and organize a meeting. Consider objectives, participants, facilities, equipment, food, agenda, and rules for the meeting.

CLB 8

You can often start a meeting by using an icebreaker activity to help people feel more comfortable. Do some online research to find ideas for icebreaker activities. In paragraph form, write about those activities that you feel would be suitable for a business meeting.

Group work

Exercise A

It is important to know how to run a successful meeting. In pairs, arrange the following steps for running a successful meeting in sequence.

1. Review the decisions made, and state who is responsible for which items.
2. Remind people of the meeting a day before.
3. Thank the attendees for their participation.
4. Keep the discussion focused.
5. Begin by clearly stating the reason for the meeting.
6. Follow the agenda. Cover the most important items in order of the priority you established.
7. Summarize the meeting. Review the decisions reached.
8. Greet people as they arrive. Start at the time stated on your agenda.
9. Manage your time. If an item needs more time, assign it to an individual or group to take care of.

Correct order: _____

Exercise B

In small groups, decide how you would handle the following difficult situations if you were the manager of a meeting.

1. A participant tries to take over the meeting or change the subject.
2. A participant gets very argumentative during a discussion.
3. During a meeting, a couple of participants are having their own side conversations about private matters.
4. A participant is very shy and not comfortable about giving his opinions in meetings.

Exercise C

You have been asked to give a presentation at a business meeting. What would you do to ensure that your talk is interesting to the participants? In small groups, discuss how you would engage your audience.

Exercise D

You will find that in any presentation given during a business meeting, speakers will use a significant number of phrasal verbs. Many phrasal verbs can be created using the words *through*, *up*, *into*, *off*, *over*, and *ahead*. Use one of these words to complete each of the following sentences.

1. Salaries almost never keep _____ with the increased cost of living.
2. The planned changes were put _____ because the committee members could not come to an agreement.
3. The members agreed to look _____ the latest statistics and try to come up with a solution.
4. The company decided not to go _____ with the plans until it had raised sufficient capital.
5. A lot of people applied for the position, but only a few turned _____ for the interview.
6. The local supermarket was recently taken _____ by a multinational company.
7. Increased spending on advertising has caused sales to pick _____
8. Sales took _____ as soon as he started production.
9. We may have to lay _____ staff if the economy doesn't pick _____.
10. The president decided to move _____ with his ideas despite the concerns of his staff.

On your own

Canadian Business Concept: Speaking well to a group is an important skill to everyone in business. You may have to present to a client, to your department, or to the entire staff at a company meeting. An excellent way to learn to speak more powerfully is to join Toastmasters, an organization that helps people feel confident speaking in public. You can find chapters in almost every city.

Search online to find your local branch of Toastmasters. Consider attending a meeting and finding out what services they provide.

Personal learning: practising English outside of the classroom

This past week I … _____

Tomorrow I will try … _____

My favourite new word is … _____

I was wondering if … _____

Before I forget, I will … _____

Answer Key

Chapter 1
Buzzwords
2. don't beat around the bush
3. do your own thing
4. time flies
5. time is money
6. out of the running

Chapter 2
Buzzwords
1. j
2. e
3. d
4. c
5. a
6. h
7. g
8. f
9. i
10. b

On your own
HR: Human Resources
CEO: Chief Executive Officer
ASAP: As Soon as Possible
ROI: Return on Investment
CPP: Canada Pension Plan
WHMIS: Workplace Hazardous Materials Information System

Chapter 3
First things first
Exercise B
1. d
2. e
3. b
4. c
5. g
6. f
7. a

Buzzwords
1. b
2. f
3. l
4. a
5. i
6. e

Vocabulary
1. same
2. different
3. different
4. same
5. different
6. different
7. different
8. different
9. different
10. same

Dialogue
1. performance review
2. bigwig
3. punch a clock
4. traffic jam
5. feedback
6. contribution
7. procedures
8. operating at warp speed
9. stressing him out
10. twiddle my thumbs
11. proactive
12. brownie points
13. office etiquette
14. slacker

Group work
Exercise A

Across / Down crossword answers:
- START OFF ON THE RIGHT FOOT
- PERFORMANCE REVIEW
- DRESS CODE
- TEAM
- JOB DESCRIPTION
- BIGWIGS
- SETUP
- SMALL TALK
- PROMOTION (PR...)
- WOULD YOU RATH... (WOULDYOURTHUMBS)
- OFFICE
- COMMUNICATION
- BROWN NOSER (BROWNOSE...)
- PROPONENT
- BOTTOM LINE
- PROUTINE
- FEEDBACK

Exercise C
1. have not seen
2. have you been
3. have been
4. have been working
5. have you been doing
6. have been selling
7. have you been doing
8. have just started

Chapter 4
First things first
Exercise E
1. T-shirt
2. sweater
3. purse
4. flip-flops
5. jeans
6. raincoat
7. pump
8. suit
9. briefcase
10. shirt
11. jacket

Buzzwords
1. b
2. a
3. e
4. f
5. h
6. c
7. g
8. d

Dialogue
1. wardrobe
2. pumps
3. over accessorize
4. fly-away hair
5. hat hair
6. business casual
7. T-shirts
8. slogan
9. wash and wear
10. trendy
11. prints
12. scent

Chapter 5
Buzzwords
1. face-to-face
2. comfort zone
3. walk the talk
4. pay lip service
5. hands-on
6. status quo
7. heartfelt

Chapter 6 Part A
Buzzwords
Exercise A
1. d
2. b
3. f
4. c
5. a
6. e
7. g

Exercise B
1. in a nutshell
2. what's up
3. get to the point
4. sink my teeth into

Group work
Exercise D

Positive Words	Negative Words	Neutral Words
thrifty	cheap	economical
classic	old-fashioned	traditional, classic
good vocal projection	loud , noisy	easily heard
verbal	chatterbox	verbal, loquacious

Chapter 6 Part B
Buzzwords
a) pay attention
b) catch on
c) on the ball
d) think outside the box
e) left in the dark
f) paper trail
g) point of view

Chapter 7
Buzzwords
1. put you through
2. hold
3. not available
4. voicemail
5. go over
6. have a moment
7. transfer
8. cut off
9. call you back
10. wrong number

Chapter 8
First things first
Exercise A
1. No
2. No
3. Yes
4. No
5. Yes
6. Yes

Exercise B

HRL and Associates

August 19, 2015

Ms Bev Smith

Event Planner
ABC Hotel
1274 Prospect Street
Toronto, ON M3A 7K2

Dear Ms Smith:

Subject: **Change to September Sales Meeting**

We reserved three conference rooms for our sales meeting on Sept. 21. We will require an extra room. Would it be possible to ensure that all four rooms are in the same area of the hotel?

We also require an LCD projector and screen for each room, and we would like to order coffee and pastries for our mid-morning break.

Please confirm that the extra room is available and that we can rent the equipment from you. Also please let us know the costs for the coffee and pastries.

Sincerely,
Patricia Oliver

(Ms) Patricia Oliver
Sales Assistant
HRL and Associates

Buzzwords
1. e
2. h
3. c
4. g
5. d
6. b
7. f
8. a

Dialogue
1. memo
2. information overload
3. concise
4. to whom it may concern
5. cordial
6. subject line
7. wordy
8. concise
9. business speak
10. natural language
11. in accordance with
12. Until such time

Group Work
Exercise B
1. g
2. j
3. a
4. i
5. b
6. c
7. d
8. f
9. h
10. e

Chapter 9
Buzzwords
Exercise A
1. e
2. a
3. d
4. c
5. b
6. f

Exercise B

1. in a bind
2. in the same boat
3. wake-up call
4. pain in the neck
5. put him down
6. play the devil's advocate

Exercise C

Negative Term	Meaning
nosy	too interested in other people's private lives
bossy	wanting control over others and telling them what to do
whiner	someone who complains about everything
nitpicker	someone who focuses on small and insignificant details
chatterbox	someone who talks continually and does not seem to want others to participate in the conversation

Chapter 10
First things first
Exercise B

1. e
2. f
3. k
4. d
5. g
6. j
7. h
8. i
9. b
10. c
11. a

Buzzwords

1. f
2. k
3. a
4. i
5. c
6. e
7. b
8. d

Vocabulary

1. assessment
2. initiative
3. probationary period
4. scrapped
5. sandwiched
6. promotion
7. criticism
8. raise

Dialogue

1. probationary period
2. high-maintenance employee
3. raise
4. heads-up
5. constructive criticism
6. sandwiched
7. promotion
8. go to bat for you
9. scrapped
10. up in arms
11. want to vent
12. connect the dots
13. pick up the slack
14. initiative
15. assessment

Chapter 11
First things first
Exercise C

1. F
2. F
3. T
4. F
5. F
6. F
7. F
8. T
9. F
10. F
11. F
12. F
13. F

Buzzwords

1. g
2. f
3. b
4. d
5. a
6. j
7. e
8. c

Vocabulary

1. inedible
2. vegetarian
3. appetizer
4. buffet
5. faux pas
6. engage

Dialogue

1. blunder
2. inedible
3. faux pas
4. table manners
5. gaffe
6. vegetarian
7. appetizer
8. engage
9. left to right
10. nibbled on it
11. cultivate
12. buffet

Group Work
Exercise A

Chapter 12
First things first
Exercise A

1. c
2. b
3. f
4. d
5. a
6. e

Exercise B

1. Verbal
2. Verbal
3. Physical
4. Non-verbal
5. Visual
6. Written
7. Physical
8. Verbal
9. Physical
10. Verbal

Buzzwords

1. c
2. l
3. e
4. a
5. m
6. i
7. g
8. j

Vocabulary

1. appease
2. flow
3. acceptable
4. inappropriate
5. apathy

Dialogue

1. grapevine
2. Don Juan
3. come on to you
4. ex
5. irks
6. sexual harrasment
7. put two and two together
8. the cat will be out of the bag
9. object of his affection

Group work
Exercise A

1. should – advice; the boss is not going to be happy with him
2. may – possibility; this man is a gossip and will repeat what you told him
3. must – certainty; this is a factual bit of information not open for discussion
4. may – possibility; Debbie had better realize that this presentation needs to happen whether she is sick or not
5. could – suggestion; don't compromise your client by taking him to a restaurant where the food is unacceptable

Chapter 13
Buzzwords

1. d
2. g
3. e
4. a
5. f
6. c
7. b

Vocabulary

1. criticism
2. criticized
3. complaints
4. prohibit
5. belittled
6. aggressive
7. appropriate
8. sarcastic
9. rude

Group work
Exercise D

1. reliable
2. hardworking
3. rude
4. cooperative
5. argumentative

Chapter 14
Buzzwords

1. c
2. a
3. f
4. e
5. b
6. g
7. d
8. h

Dialogue

1. networking
2. host
3. connect
4. event
5. socializing
6. forge
7. align
8. mingle

Chapter 15
Buzzwords

1. workaholics
2. mission impossible
3. to-do list
4. pros and cons
5. keep your eye on the ball
6. missed the boat
7. on the back burner

Chapter 16
First things first
Exercise A

Job Title	Job Description	Tip
Porter	Carries your luggage at the airport or on a train	$1 per bag
Doorman	Handles the arrivals and departures of guests and gets you a taxi when you step out	$1 to $3
Bellhop	Takes luggage from the car or taxi and delivers it to your room	$1 per bag
Concierge	Acts as a resource who responds to guests' needs	$5 to $10 for making reservations or getting tickets
Taxi driver	Drives you wherever you want to go within the city	10 to 15 percent of your fare
Room service attendant	Brings meals to your hotel room	15 to 20 percent of the value of items delivered
Valet parking attendant	Parks your car	$2 per day

Exercise B

1. h	4. a	7. c
2. d	5. e	8. f
3. b	6. g	

Buzzwords

1. a	4. g	7. d
2. j	5. e	8. k
3. c	6. h	

Vocabulary

1. expenses	4. dress code	7. itinerary
2. facilities	5. tipsy	8. compensate
3. mini-bar	6. receipts	

Dialogue

1. fiasco	4 mini-bar	7. ate and ran
2. dress code	5. tipsy	8. BYO
3. pigging out	6. talking shop	9. wet blanket

Chapter 17
First things first
Exercise A

1. c	5. f
2. e	6. g
3. d	7. a
4. b	

Buzzwords

1. a	4. f	7. g
2. l	5. d	8. i
3. j	6. b	

Dialogue

1. ramble off on another topic
2. lose track
3. accent
4. brought something to the table
5. wrap up
6. droned on
7. engage
8. teleconference
9. voice distractors

Group work
Exercise A
Correct order: 2, 8, 5, 6, 9, 4, 1, 7, 3

Exercise D

1. up	5. up	9. off, up
2. off	6. over	10. ahead
3. into	7. up	
4. ahead	8. off	

Photograph Credits